FORCED
TO
FLY

EDITED AND COMPILED BY

JOANNA PARFITT

'From quiet homes and first beginning,
Out to the undiscovered ends,
There's nothing worth the wear of winning,
But laughter and the love of friends.'

Hilaire Belloc

SUMMERTIME PUBLISHING

SUMMERTIME PUBLISHING

Published in 1998 by Summertime Publishing
The Old Stables, Geeston, Stamford, Lincs, PE9 3RH
Tel/Fax: (44) (0)1780–480304
Mobile: (44) 0403 622468
email: summertime@lineone.net

Produced in Quark XPress 3.3 by Joanna Parfitt and Natasha Hurley-Walker
Jacket Design, Production and Layout Advice by
Plus Two Design, Frognall, Lincs
Cover illustration by Patrick Blower
Incidental artwork by Jenny Gosling, Anne Hetmaniak,
Jennifer Loos, Karis A Loos and Laura Westbury

Editorial Contributions – Karen Bird, Elizabeth Douet, Claire Ellis, Linda March
Proof Reading and Editing – Elizabeth Douet, Jennifer Gosling, Peter Gosling,
Natasha Hurley-Walker, Marion Malone, Linda March, Bobby Meyer

Printed in Great Britain by Wayzgoose

ISBN 0 9529453 20

LETTER FROM THE SPONSOR

It is a pleasure to contribute to *Forced to Fly* on behalf of Schlumberger families around the world. As more and more of us find ourselves uprooting, moving and reorientating to another location every few years, we need, and fall gratefully upon, a book like this – packed with positive suggestions and effective solutions.

Forced to Fly complements the ideals of the Schlumberger Spouses Association perfectly: we aim to provide similar, informal support for all Schlumberger families around the world. Each family gives and receives as much or as little as it needs depending upon nationality, background and personal inclination. We have generated so much fun and enthusiasm in only five years since conception, that we now have over sixty locations around the globe.

The Schlumberger Spouses Association is run by and for spouse-volunteers, as we all aim to "soften each others' landings" wherever we find ourselves. Our informal network of friendship, fun and support embraces over forty nationalities in as many countries. We have the full support from Schlumberger itself, moral and financial, as well as access to the Company intranet, and, increasingly, our own website with local webpages packed with crucial information about housing, schools and local living standards. As the partnership between spouse-volunteers and Company Personnel matures, we are benefitting from a galaxy of in-Company initiatives such as personal security seminars, financial planning advice, first aid and defensive driving courses – all tailored to each location and the specific needs of the local Schlumberger community of families.

So, anything is possible if you have support and do not feel too alone. Forced to fly you may be . . . but once you reach cruising altitude you will find others there with you. So go for it! Have a laugh, turn all those near disasters into great stories, focus on the absurdity of those numerous dramas and enter into the good humour of this book as part of your essential state-of-mind for life on the move.

Good luck.

Fiona Warner

Schlumberger Spouses Association
Global Co-ordinator

CONTENTS

Another Suitcase Another Long Haul, Peter Gosling
Rain, Terri Nagel
Driving me Mad, Joanna Parfutt
Stick it Out, Carol Mackenzie
Bellydance, Gurpreet Tirwana
Telly Addicts, Mark Eadie
Wife at Large in Paris, Louise Rankin
All Part of the Service, Joanna Parfitt
Flying Tales, Jean Exbrayat
Getting to Know You, Mark Eadie
Finding My Ski Legs, Linda March
The Carpenter Came to Call, Sue Valentine
Jacques in the Box, Sandra Williamson
Housegirls Make You Fat, Joanna Parfitt
The Fine Art of Haggling, Mark Eadie
Minding Language, Christine Yates
Norsk Trouble, Paul Cleary
Kissing and the Art of Keeping Friends, Joanna Parfitt
Saving Mangoes, Gurpreet Tirwana
Recording it All, Mark Eadie
The Horror of Holidays, Joanna Parfitt
Norwegian Holiday, Elizabeth Douet
Dinner Party Disasters, Elise Allen

Departure Lounge

FOREWORD

I once attended a workshop given by a much travelled psychotherapist to a group of fellow expatriates. She talked of the grief experienced by us all as we move from country to country. We leave behind friends, support and all that is familiar. Then she went on to explain her personal theory about expatriate wives in particular. That they are 'forced to fly'.

In a matter of days or weeks we have to sell off, wind down and say goodbye to one place and come to terms with another. We have to find schools, accommodation, supermarkets, friends, social life, doctors . . . the list is endless.

So why do we do it? We do it because of the compensations. Because of the wonderful people we meet along the way. The experiences. Different cultures. Adventure. The silk in Thailand; saki in Japan; steaks in the States. We do it for the good times and the opportunities. We also have the tremendous advantage of knowing that, chances are, we will get the chance to leave all the bad bits behind again.

Moving on means that we get the chance to clean up our acts. Time to turf out the lidless freezer boxes and broken toys. Time to pack only the essentials. We can just about live without a teapot but woe betide any family member who forgets to pack his or her sense of humour!

One of the best things about being an expatriate wife is the huge support and help that is available from fellow trailing spouses. People have either given me their help for free, or else we have bartered skills. I do not know of another set of people quite so generous.

Forced to Fly was compiled to provide some of the help and support you need when you land on foreign soil. Part One will give you the inspiration and practical advice that can help towards an effective life on the move. Part Two provides some light relief in the form of humorous accounts written by men and women expatriates everywhere.

This anthology could never have been compiled without the voluntary contributions of other expatriates. I would like to thank all of you for your efforts and patience, particularly Patrick Blower, cartoonist for The Evening Standard, for the cover, to Anne, Jennifer, Karis, Laura and my mother, Jenny, for their incidental artwork and also the many expatriates who eventually succumbed to my nagging and wrote something. Finally my thanks go to my husband, Ian and children Sam and Josh, who have learned to live with my creativity and an untidy home. Owing to the cosmopolitan nature of this book we have decided to use American or English spellings as appropriate to each contributor.

Thanks to the talents and generosity of the international community and the Schlumberger Spouses Association, who have underwritten the printing costs, *Forced to Fly* was able to fly. It is your book.

Joanna Parfitt, Editor

Coping With Culture Shock
by
Linda March

Linda was on the move for most of her childhood. When, at last, she thought she had settled down in England, her family was posted to Norway.

For the first time in my life I felt truly at home. After a nomadic service childhood and then moves associated with university, jobs, career changes and marriage, I was now firmly established in the place I wanted to be: a Victorian home which was finally just the way we wanted, only 10 minutes from the seafront.

Our two little girls were happily settled in the school at which I had until recently been teaching. Many of the staff were personal friends and had known my girls since they'd seen the first twinkle in my eye and bulge in my waistband. I had a doctor who knew my name and who had been there at both deliveries. After years of nightmare experiences I had found the best dentist in the world and if I ever had a bad hair day then an appointment with Helen could fix it. My weekly shopping at Waitrose took half the morning because the aisles were an obstacle course of people from church, ex colleagues, mothers of children I had taught and, of course, friends who could tempt me out of the morning's plans and into the coffee shop. I knew the short cuts to avoid the traffic from here to there across town and, most importantly, I knew where everything and everyone was – where to look for a widget, where to find out about ballet lessons, the best child-friendly restaurants, whom to call when the house was suddenly and inexplicably invaded by flying insects. So, yes, for the first time in my life I felt truly settled. Then, if you've picked up this book you will guess what happened – I was forced to fly. To Norway as a trailing spouse (although I was at that time thankfully unaware of my unflattering new title).

To tell the truth I was a bit miffed. To tell the real truth I was beside myself with rage! Furious with my husband for 'making' us go, 'making' us leave our lovely home for some horrible cold place miles from anywhere, despite his constant offers to turn the job down if it was going to make me this unhappy; resenting his company for making him an offer that was too good to turn down; afraid of how I would cope in a strange environment; deeply saddened at leaving old friends and family and heartbroken at the prospect of wrenching my daughters from their nearby beloved grandmother.

And so the nightmare began. For weeks the walls of our home reverberated with yells or pure silence as we alternated between fighting and not speaking. Then John departed to find a house for us and an office for the new Norwegian branch of his company and so, with a heavy heart, a churning stomach and a feeling that I was powerless to control my fate, I organised the million and one things that have to be done before beginning an international move - sorting out, throwing out, crying, packing up, informing the world and his wife of our unpronounceable new address, crying, finding tenants for my lovely home, crying and saying endless goodbyes.

The 360 mile drive to Newcastle in high winds with a tarpaulin flying free as the rope holding it in place over the roof rack luggage worked loose and necessitated stops every few miles, was conducted mostly in tears. The 19 hour ferry crossing in the same high winds was spent mostly with my head in a sick bag, perversely grateful that the girls were also sick otherwise I would never have coped had they wanted to leave the cabin. John had offered to meet us at Stavanger harbour but as our new home was apparently only 10 minutes away and as the car was stacked to the gunwales with everything we might need to make us, and particularly the children, feel at home until our shipment arrived,

I'd told him not to bother. I'd blithely asked him just to give me directions – I was bound to be able to find it – I'd managed the first million miles of the journey without help, I was pretty sure I could manage the last seven kilometres.

And if I thought the nightmare had begun, well I was really in for a shock. John's new position setting up an office in Norway meant that we were completely alone. There was no big company, foreign service or military organisation behind us. We had no-one to meet us, show us the ropes, invite us for coffee and thrust a welcome pack in our hands. We were on our own and although Norway is not, on the surface, so culturally different from the UK, and despite the fact that so many Norwegians speak excellent English, as complete strangers we just didn't know where to begin. Nine days after our arrival John went offshore to work and, if three months previously I had felt truly settled for the first time in my life, now I felt truly abandonned for the first time in my life, particularly as a nagging stomach pain grew worse and worse. Two days later I found myself in a foreign hospital suffering from excruciatingly painful kidney stones . . . (read *Sick in Stavanger* later in this book)

. . . 15 months later sitting in one of our favourite restaurants in Stavanger with my mother, who was on one of her regular visits, the girls broke off from their excited description of their previous weekend's skiing trip and their insistence that Grandma should come to see them ice skating the next day, to wave to school friends who had just walked in. As I confidently translated the menu for her, my mother suddenly exclaimed proudly, 'You've done it, Linda, you've made a new life for your family.' I gazed out at the familiar harbour and felt a surge of pride too. Yes, I had done it, but the journey from the hospital to the restaurant was a long one, via a deep dark tunnel that began with severe culture shock and ended with successful coping strategies.

Culture Shock: What is it?

In *Moving and Living Abroad*, Albright, Cho and Austin identify the 'typical expatriate morale curve'. They suggest that the pre-departure and very early arrival stage is often a peak honeymoon period, characterised by 'enthusiasm, sociability and self-confidence – and ignorance of real cultural differences'. This is followed by the trough of despair, a time when you start to hate everything and everyone. This is true culture shock. You feel alone, ostracised even, and this can last for weeks, or months, until signs of adaptation and peaks of contentment appear. This final stage, when you can at last leave behind the limbo of transition, is called integration. Although stressful periods can occur at any time during an overseas assignment, it is generally agreed that the period of maximum stress usually occurs in the first year.

Oh dear, so culture shock really exists. Does that mean we all have to take a ride on this emotional roller coaster every time we face a location move? I'm afraid so, but let's be positive, there may be low spots but there are also highs. And one important thought to hold on to when you're hurtling down into the depths of culture shock is that others have hurtled as you are hurtling now. They have felt what you are feeling and they understand. You are not weak, inadequate, pathetic or going round the twist. You are passing though a phase we all have to go through and, like the terrible twos and teenage pimples, it's a phase you will leave behind. The light at the end of the tunnel is, in the findings of Albright, Cho and Austin, that '[Culture shock] is a profound learning experience, which can lead to a great degree of self-awareness and personal growth. The growth may take time and may be painful, but the results are usually worth it'. In my opinion they are well worth it.

I'm pleased to hear that many people experience a honeymoon period on arrival in their new location. My strong negative attitude to moving meant that I went straight to jail without collecting £200 – straight to that time when the honeymoon's over, when culture shock steps in. Culture shock is a very personal experience. For me it manifested itself in the million different ways in which everything was different.

To the friendly outgoing Texan, whose back garden gate opened onto a well worn path round the beautiful Norwegian fjord, culture shock was wrapped up in the way Norwegians walked stonily past without an acknowledgement, far less a cheery smile.

To the British mother of two young boys, at her wit's end during a cold, rainy half term holiday who telephoned the local Tourist office to find out if any children's activities were laid on that week it was being told to take them shopping because some of the shops had Lego tables.

Your new home may be a hotel, a tiny flat in an inhospitable block assigned to aliens; it may be surrounded by armed guards; it may be bigger and better than the one you've come from. In some foreign postings it may even contain servants who attend to your every need, but whatever it is, it isn't home – at least not yet. You're in the grip of culture shock because everything is different and everyone is different. If you just go over the hill or round the corner you won't see a familiar landmark and get your bearings. That tall red headed figure you caught sight of out of the corner of your eye isn't your best friend. Your heart sinks at the realisation that there's no one to laugh with about that awful incident in the supermarket this morning: your attempt to peek and discover whether the bag that held what felt and sounded like oats actually contained oats, resulted in a splitting sound and a floor strewn with split peas.

Just moving to a new location in your own country where you understand the language and culture is difficult enough – you know you need to go to Boots the Chemist, but you still have to find where Boots is, but it's even harder when everything around you is strange and there's no Boots to go to. And in very foreign locations your senses may be assailed by different smells, sounds, light and colours. However, the foreigness of the location is not always an indication of the level of culture shock.

One British multi-mover remarked that despite having lived in the very different and austere locations of Russia and Azerbaijan, she suffered more culture shock in locations closer to home, like France and Norway, simply because others expected that she would instantly cope and so no-one offered help. In far flung locations the expatriate network is usually highly developed.

Every day has a million problems and the local equivalent of the Yellow Pages telephone directory doesn't hold the answer. What is the Norwegian/ Thai/Spanish/Russian for hairdresser/exhaust fitter/urine infection/sultanas? Everyday tasks take for ever and how and where do you do them? How do you feed your finicky family with unrecognisable cuts of meat, a limited or bizarre choice of vegetables and fruit that costs four times as much as it would at home? You find yourself carrying about your own desert island as you tune out of the world around you because you can't understand conversations, signs, headlines, radio. And, on a day when you can't find the chicken stock cubes and resort, exhausted to accosting a cashier and doing an impersonation of a chicken while drawing a square box on the back of an envelope, it can tip you over edge.

And of course, everyone else is doing just fine. Your new world is peopled with confident, coping, outgoing women for whom moving from one side of the world to another is just a breeze. They all have wonderful social lives, successful children (well, they would have: they're all perfect mothers) and hundreds of friends. At least that's the way it seems to you. They seem to be laughing down at you from the top of the mountain. You, meanwhile, are stuck on the starting slopes. Anyway, they're not your sort. And so isolation begins.

Homesickness

Well, of course, everything at home was better. Everyone at home was better. You don't want any new friends, you want your old ones. It goes without saying how much you miss the company of friends and family, but it can be quite surprising to discover just how much you miss acquaintances and places. I inexplicably missed the enterprising young lad who used to sell and deliver my bin bags and who always had a tale to tell of his girlfriend and his daughter on his fortnightly appearances at my door. And there's another thing, as one woman in the throes of homesickness remarked, 'The door bell never rings and I never open the door to find a friend standing there.'

Transition and Coping with Change

It makes sense to try and be as prepared as possible for your new location and your new life – doing your homework in advance, having a contact to call on, psyching up your children, maybe taking a pre-move reconnaissance trip, but however prepared you are you will still have to go through the transition of really saying goodbye to one place and being in another. From the first news that you are moving until you are sitting in that favourite restaurant, you are in limbo. Limbo and transition are lengthy and painful, but take heart, where there are endings there are also beginnings.

If easy things like buying bread are hard to cope with in your new location, then hard things are even harder to cope with. Moving to a new location is a significant change in our lives, but other changes are happening all the time too. Most multi-movers are moving around at stages in their lives when there are many other important changes: career changes for themselves or their partner, the birth of children, new schools, illness or even death of relatives far away back home.

Katherine Prendergast, an American psychotherapist working on a Family Crisis Intervention Team and herself an international mover, has seen the following phenomena many, many times.

'Crises, life changes or transitions seem to come in groups of three – almost a ripple effect. Most of us handle the first crisis and even the second relatively well. But it is the third crisis which seems to put us over the edge. We have used up our emotional and physical energy and strength dealing with the first two crises – there's little left for the third. This is when we need the help and support of our family, friends and professionals to help us cope and successfully move on,' Katherine explains.

In a new location family and friends aren't there and you have no idea where to go for professional help when you can't speak the language or understand how the health system works.

Making a New Life

Let's face it, as trailing spouse, you're the one who is going to have to do it. The likelihood is that your partner will just swap one office for another with the same company logo, same computer system, and only a lighter or heavier weight suit to deal with (poor darling). If a real new life is to be built then you are going to have to lay the foundation stones – but they can be heavy bricks to carry so give yourself time. It's okay to have a bad day, a bad week, a bad month, but it's not okay to hibernate for ever. Be gentle with yourself as you would with your children, feel sorry for yourself – you've had a hard day discovering that self raising flour doesn't exist here, the oven is useless and that your best recipe cake that is guaranteed to cheer everyone up has hardened into a piece of local granite. But, just as after a reasonable amount of time you would coax a recalcitrant youngster out of his room, coax yourself out into the world. It's time to fill your time, to make friends, to get involved.

Ask for Help

If you need help – and you are going to need help – then ask for it. If you're on your own without the safety net of a large organisation then ask a friendly mum who said 'hello' in the school playground. The odds are that she's a recovering culture shock victim, will remember what it's like and help. And if she doesn't, then ask someone else. Keep asking – you'll probably get the chance to return the favour before too long.

When I slid on a pool of water in the bathroom and heard the crack of my ankle bone I just knew I was going to need help. Over the next two months, as I worked my way back to mobility, the contents of my kitchen cupboards became as familiar to the mothers of my children's classmates as my children became to the insides of their cars. Like Tennessee Williams' Blanche I had to rely on the kindness of strangers and their kindness overwhelmed me. Most of my 'thank you's' were met with, 'Well, it could happen to any of us, we're all in the same boat with no old friends and family to call on.'

Say Yes

The advice of another much mobile wife and mother who seemed to adjust remarkably quickly to her new surroundings was, 'accept any invitations offered'. And when they're offered, fix a date and time, don't leave it hanging vaguely in mid-air, you'll lose the impetus or courage and never get round to ringing. Don't wait too long to take that step towards friendship.

Conventional behaviour at home might make you wait several months or even years before developing a friendship – nodding at the gate for three months, progressing to 'Good morning' for another three and then eventually asking how the children are. In this way it can be years before you move on to real friendship or an invitation to dinner. In your new life your fellow friendly expat will have moved on to pastures new in that time and you may have missed the chance of a beautiful friendship. It's sad if you find out at their leaving party that you had so much in common and could have been good friends, so don't let the grass grow under your feet.

There's no two ways about it: unless you are a complete loner, then to be tolerably happy you are going to have to make friends. One way to do that is to accept all invitations.

But what if none come? Then you have to make the moves. However, if the thought of hoving up to a room or playground of complete strangers, whose only connection with you is that they come from the same country or have children in the same class as yours, and saying a cheery, 'Hi everyone, I'm Linda!' fills you with horror, then find more natural ways to get to know people. The old ones are the best: join groups, societies, sign up to help sew the costumes for the school

Christmas play. An offer of help works wonders and gives you a purpose to be there, a role, a natural way to relate to others. Accept everything – if you end up doing too much at least you'll be busy and the phone will ring. You can always offload when you've had time to work out what you really want to spend your time doing.

Being forced out of your safe, cosy routine is scary. It can be traumatic to face 7.30 on a Monday evening without Coronation Street after a lifetime of its companionship, but the change will make you shake yourself up. Maybe there's something else you could do that you've never thought of. Now is the time to try.

Children

The good news is that so called Third Culture Kids – born in one country, moved to another, and calling yet another home are the citizens who will fit into the 21st century's mobile world. The bad news is that, like you, they may have to go through that deep dark tunnel to get there. The worse news is that you may have to put up with tantrums, bad dreams and bed wetting on the journey. Different ages will, of course, have different problems – teenagers, for whom fitting in is vital, will probably refuse to go without giving you hell. Little ones may react to the upheaval by refusing to let you out of their sight. Accept your children and their reactions. Remember that you are the constant in their lives and try to create as much stability as possible. Prepare them for the changes and keep the channels of communication open. Help create memories for them.

Much-moved Carlanne Herzog, who is a Professional Cultural Trainer, advises photographing the real places you see and use everyday – the school playground, the grocery shop. We tend to take our cameras on the once in a lifetime trips up mountains, rivers or monuments. But the places we and our children will really want to be reminded of are the everyday places that made up our lives in this location.

I recently met Joanna, a five year old who had moved to Singapore from Jakarta for a month during the troubles. When we met she was on summer holiday in England. She asked if I would like to see her 'school book' from Singapore and showed me a simple A4 sheaf of stapled papers. Her class teacher had pasted photographs of the pupils and the daily routines and photocopied them. 'This is where we wash our hands after play time' and 'first we put our reading folders in Miss White's basket' and so on were among the descriptions. To Joanna this book was vitally important and provided a link to her current reality.

Remember that it's as important for your child to say his or her goodbyes as it is for you. Why not let your child hand out pre-addressed, pre-stamped postcards to his school friends. In that way he is sure to be remembered for a while.

Let your child know a little of how you are feeling. Don't be too over enthusiastic about your new location. Children need to know that it is okay to express their emotions. If you show you are sad, they can be sad too.

Visitors and Home Visits

Your new location may be glamorous, sunny, warm – the ideal holiday spot. Before you leave you say, 'Come and see us,' and people that you previously would spend an evening with now blow their life savings to travel half way round the world to spend two weeks holiday with you. And you had never realised just how awful their children were. Your visitors often assume that because they are on holiday you are on holiday.

This is not necessarily the case. You may be trying to keep piano lessons, Brownies and homework going in between acting as a local guide, gourmet cook and wine drinker extraordinaire. And you still have to get up at the crack of dawn to fill lunch boxes and do the school run. A service wife stationed at a particularly desirable holiday location recalls one incoming batch of visitors spending their first night on the floor while they waited for the previous batch to depart. Her life, when she wasn't at her full time job, was a whirl of sheet changing and laundry.

Visitors are wonderful, especially in the early days. A friendly face from home to explore your new location with and to really talk to is a real joy. But living in each other's pockets for too long can add a strain. Be aware and learn to take a deep breath. Help your visitors to be as independent as possible so that they can take themselves off to see the local 'must' of a tourist site. There's a limit to how many times you can 'ooh' and 'aah' at the same relic.

The stress of too many people cooped up together in the same house can also arise on home visits. An answer may be to rent a holiday home and hire a car for the duration. This gives you the freedom of your own base and own mobility and the option to invite people to come to you instead of spending your entire home leave on the motorway from friends to parents to distant uncle. It also enables your children to react to their reverse culture shock like complete brats without it being constantly on display to others.

A few more don'ts for home visits:

Don't go home too soon, it can be very unsettling and your return journey can drop you right back into those uncomfortable first feelings of culture shock.

And, in my opinion, avoid the unspeakable madness of travelling half way round the world alone with small children. If your spouse really, truly can't travel with you then he should either be shot at dawn or prepared to shell out for someone to accompany you. An American expatriate wife faced with undertaking the long haul and three changes of aircraft between Stavanger and New

Orleans alone, just knew she would lose one of her three youngsters in an airport so offered her sister an expenses paid holiday in beautiful Norway providing she undertook the return journey with them.

Once home try and avoid the even greater madness of buying everything in sight. On my first trip home I almost burst into tears in the Waitrose supermarket. Such clearly, cleanly, beautifully laid out goods, such choice, such prices! I felt as if I was in Aladdin's cave and wanted to buy everything. Similar feelings are aroused in many familiar stores. Whether you are arriving home from an extremely expensive country so that everything at home is half the price, or from a country where you just cannot get the goods you need, take a deep breath before you buy too many things that are just 'might come in handies'. They just might not and will be a headache to get rid of when you're clearing out for your next move in two years' time.

Reverse Culture Shock

Your return home, either for a visit or for repatriation, can throw you into reverse culture shock. You have to learn to live with your own people again, people who don't have your newly acquired breadth of experience.

Homecoming expectations can cause another large peak as the assignment comes to an end (that is if you are, by then, happy to be going home), but the thrill of repatriation is often countered by the realism of friends and relatives who are uninterested in your experience. You may find a new job that does not take advantage of your new skills, if you can find a job at all. You may find that your confidence takes a hammering too.

Carlanne Herzog, whose training courses include the tellingly titled, 'So you think you're going home?', points out, 'While culture shock is caused by loss of the familiar, re-entry shock is when we have changed and the familiar no longer works for us. Successful overseas adjustments become repatriation challenges.' But that is another book!

When you emerge from the tunnel

The long winter of your first year is over, the sun is shining, there's a hint of promise in the air, the phone is ringing and there are entries on the calendar. You've accepted your location and you've somehow found yourself on the school's Parents' Committee and in the cross stitching circle. It doesn't matter that you can't sew, you're involved. Remember what it was like and give those following you in the tunnel a helping hand and a gentle tug. Say hello, ask a new woman for coffee, invite her children to play. Yours might be the only friendly face she's seen that day, that week, and your encouraging words can make all the difference. I so remember the many small acts of kindness (life-changingly great to me) from kind women who are up for canonisation in my eyes. The life of multi-movers is a constant rolling cycle. Take what you know and pass it on.

Linda would like to recommend the following publications :

Culture Shock! A Parent's Guide
Robin Pascoe
Times
ISBN 185733 0722

Culture Shock! A Wife's Guide
Robin Pascoe
Times
ISBN 185733 1966

Moving and Living Abroad
Albright, Cho and Austin
Hippocrene Books
ISBN 078180048x

Especial thanks to Katherine Prendergast and Carlanne Herzog

Making the Most of Your Host Country
by
Claire Ellis

Claire is an Australian, currently living in Jakarta. She has written for the Culture Shock series and is particularly interested in environmental research.

Moving overseas to a new location can be a richly rewarding experience full of new opportunities and challenges which evokes envy from friends and compatriots at home. Years later, thoughts of your foreign assignments will bring back a wealth of warm, fond memories and funny stories. This seemingly ideal view ends up being true for the majority of people who choose to re-locate overseas for work.

But at the time the moving process can be very difficult and emotionally draining. A new posting, particularly in the first year, creates problems that need to be acknowledgeᴜ and overcome, not ignored. Any stay can be made enjoyable or frustrating. It takes effort and the right mental attitude to settle into a new place and there are ways of making the adjustment smoother and faster.

Creating and settling into a new home, finding friends, sharing laughter over daily details and making the most of the new location are crucial in the process. Make yourself useful and contribute as well as take.

Every country and place has its good and bad sides. Nowhere is perfect, not even home. The key to being happy is going with an open mind. Be flexible: treat it as a new set of opportunities and not 'lost time'.

Of course, every place is different. I have had two postings in Jakarta totalling six years. A city of 11m people with over 50,000 expats, it has a vast array of clubs and groups catering for the needs of expats. Everything from an Australia New Zealand Association, Korean Club and Spanish Speaking group, to St Patrick's Balls and a St David's Society. The list is enormous but most importantly, they have expatriate community centres specifically designed to help newcomers get orientated to their new life as well as provide fun for those already settled.

By contrast, I have also lived in Vietnam during the relatively early stages of it opening up to foreigners. Within a short time we knew every expatriate in town. Housing, schooling and health care were extremely basic or virtually non-existent. Add to this a tonal language that was impossible for me to wrap my tongue around and you can imagine the culture shock I experienced. The choice of friends and activities was extremely limited so we made our own fun.

Undoubtedly, some places are easier to adjust to than others and it is difficult to generalise. But some of the toughest ones, the most different from home, turn out to be the most rewarding. Moving creates a rich range of new experiences and opportunities but you have to reach out and find and choose the right ones for you.

Take your treasures with you

Home is a place of refuge, your spot to relax and unwind and feel safe. A few possessions and a little effort can turn any room into a short or long term home. Think about this when you pack. Your shipment may take several months to arrive at your new destination, or you may be in hotel accommodation for months waiting for a suitable house to become available. Take a few small possessions in your suitcase for this interim period. It may be as simple as a favourite coffee mug and a couple of framed photos of the family. Even a hotel room can have your own stamp on it.

Any friend is better than no friend

It is very important for you to make new friends and settle into the new place. But this is not always easy, particularly in small locations. The challenge makes you suddenly realise that no-one ever teaches you the most efficient way to identify and make friends. These new associates are not replacements for the rich friendships developed over years you still have at home (and try not to judge them by those standards), but for the moment they are equally important. These people understand what you are going through as you adjust to your new location and are there to share a laugh, give assistance and advice. As always, the informal network is the best place to find answers to everything and anything from hiring a new computer whiz at work, to finding a favourite restaurant and dealing in a culturally acceptable manner with a maid who is stealing from you. Everyone needs friends and becoming an active member of your new community is a crucial part of the settling in process.

Being Australian, many of the people I bond fastest with are other Australians. It's natural as we share the same language, sense of humour, culture and background and can exchange news from home easily. I always join an Australian group at each new posting if it exists. However to only make Australian friends or even other expat friends means I would have effectively cut myself off from the very country and people I am living in. I could have missed out on the rich wealth of information and variety of cross-cultural friendships that are such an important part of the overseas experience. Expatriate organisations are enclaves and wonderful havens at times, but those people best adapted to their new home find ways to truly integrate, to fit across the cross cultural gaps and make friends with local people too. Don't forget the rich mixture of other nationalities that also may be expatriate in the same community. The new life you create for yourself should be a balanced reflection of life in your new locale.

Don't treat your assignment as a waiting room

Some people accept a two or three year posting and return home afterwards, but many others, while intending to only be away for a few years, end up overseas for many more. Interestingly, statistics show a significant number choose not to settle back in their original home. Even a short term stay can be fun, and a valuable learning experience. Treating it as too short a time to be of use, or by clinging to your last home instead of settling into the new one, often leads to unhappiness. Mentally staying attached to the last home defers, or prevents, you making this new one a home.

It is tempting, when possible, to zip back to your roots regularly to keep in touch with your 'real' home. This can be a lovely luxury and there are times in our lives when it becomes necessary, for instance, to help a sick relative or to oversee home renovations and so on. However, it can also become a trap, not allowing you to settle into the new location. Being away for extended periods naturally disrupts your activities in your new location. It is mentally difficult to be attached to two places and two sets of people and activities at once. Avoid returning home too much. Stay involved, maintain friendships and become part of the social life in your new home.

Do something you care about

I started as a newly arrived lost soul in Jakarta and volunteered in the local Friends of the Zoo program. One thing led to another. At first I was making speeches on the Indonesian animals and environment . Later I was offered a job as a lecturer on an Indonesian cruise ship, which turned out to be the most exclusive of its kind in the country and ran soft adventure trips. I ended up working for them for seven years part time in a dream job that is never advertised. Later I wrote a book on one of the areas we sailed through. Life, and finding work, is evolutionary!!!

Once you arrive, the first few months are hectic. It takes time and energy learning your way around, absorbing a new language and culture, settling into new routines and lifestyles and trying to make and find a home. It all sounds like hard work but much of it can be fascinating and fun.

Turn shopping into a cultural experience

Shopping, for instance, is an essential task but also can be much more. Heading out into the markets is a great learning experience. They are a place to practice your language and bargaining skills, and to observe some of the customs and habits of the people. For instance, in China, the best time for a good price may be the first sale of the day as they believe the fortunes of the rest of the day rest on this. Food markets are colourful bustling revelations of the pulse of everyday life. Learn what is grown in each season and where. Sellers are only too willing to give you tips on how to cook or prepare any unusual foods.

Exploring the handicraft markets is equally fascinating and often less smelly. Pick up some cheap bargains to help decorate the new house or to use as presents to send back home, each with a special story of discovery attached. Chatting with sellers tell you how they are made, what they are made of, how they were used and the culture of the people who make them. The reasons for subtle quality variations become clear. Research past there and go and visit the artisans themselves to see how it's done. This gets you away from tourist sites and you start to see and learn about the real country and how people live.

Antique shopping also is an enjoyable quick way to make the history of the country come alive. The more you delve into the variations in styles and types of products, the more you learn.

Scanning the markets for treasures can become much more than an idle pastime. Friends have used their proximity to the producers to become immersed. Several I know have written Masters or PhD theses on cloth motifs and the role of various artefacts in tribal beliefs. Others have set up an export business, helping local artisans get a better income while meeting the demand for well-made, unusual handicrafts back home. Another runs gourmet cooking classes and sells speciality dishes, having developed good relationships with local suppliers and chefs. Take slides and offer to lecture on something that interests you or write magazine articles. All sorts of ideas may emerge.

If shopping isn't your idea of fun, there are many other ways to learn about your new home. Museums and zoos often have volunteer programs. Many charity associations also welcome help and are a way of becoming involved, teaching you at the same time about the social structure, issues and problems of the country.

Spread your wings a little

Plan travel trips with friends and start to explore the country. Other newcomers are probably just as keen to have a travel companion as you and sharing the organisation makes it easier. Alternatively, link in with experienced friends or a cultural or museum group that explores the local country, people and culture as part of their activities. Getting away and out of home can be a wonderful break and it reveals the fascinating natural, historical and cultural attractions of the new country. It also means when guests from overseas come to visit, you can be the knowledgeable travel guide or advisor.

Break down barriers

Barriers are often built on more than just language issues and the extent to which they exist varies dramatically from country to country, and even within countries, between racial groups. The reasons for them are many. Take time to understand why they are there, as only then is it possible to work around them. For instance, when I lived in Vietnam, it was during the early days of opening up the communist country to westerners. The people had had years of powerful political messages warning against westerners and our culture. We were also watched carefully by the secret police to check we were not stirring up dissent or spreading politically subversive messages. Naturally, many Vietnamese were reluctant to mix with westerners unless it was for a legitimate business dealing. At the other extreme are cultural groups who have been exposed to foreigners within their country for generations and are simply not very interested in us any more. They frequently consider it not worth the effort to make deep friendships as we may not be staying in their country for more than a few years. The reasons for barriers are numerous and are frequently complex overlays of religious, social and cultural bias.

An interest in the produce of a country or an involvement in volunteer organisations can be useful aids to get you past initial barriers but there are other non-threatening, acceptable ways to start getting to know the local people. Offer to teach or tutor conversational language classes. You might be employed or choose to do it on a voluntary basis for a company, at school, in private classes or for children in their own home. This latter choice may appear inconvenient but being invited into someone's home on a regular basis again gives you a chance to observe many other aspects of their lives and develop friendships.

Seek out the silver lining

Learn to accept and concentrate on the positive aspects of your host country. Consciously note the ways you may have grown and expanded since you moved overseas. It is not easy. For instance, my finely honed skills of pushing through the wet markets of Vietnam in local fashion were not appreciated in my quiet home town of Tasmania where more than three people constitutes a crowd. But Vietnam also taught me how to recognise unlabelled cuts of meat and my severely tested skills of food substitution means I can whip up a meal out of virtually anything . My 'east meets west' food combinations talked about in fancy recipe books were learnt at the basic level as I had no choice.

It is not easy, particularly in the beginning. There are going to be bad days. After all, who is so perfect and lucky they don't have bad days at home too? Accept that juggling two homes, friends and a family spread around the world while perhaps also bringing up children in a new environment, is tough.

I must admit I hadn't really thought about all this until about six months into my first overseas posting. A lady, who had arrived around the same time as me in the same company as my husband, packed up and left, quitting the country and her husband, saying it wasn't worth it. I missed her as we had done quite a bit together, but I also felt strangely better. A much more travelled individual nodded wisely and said to me 'Don't let other people drag you down. Be careful of making friends with people who are always negative. It's like an insidious disease that is contagious and drags you down too.'

Acknowledge that you have given up a lot in the uprooting and moving process and make sure there are some paybacks for you. Build in treats. Make the most of the luxuries available. Have a massage. Try reflexology. Find a way to relax and let the problems and hassles go by (see chapter entitled *How to Be Happy – Naturally*). Friends and laughter are two of the best.

While the initial months taken settling down tend to be quite hectic, most spouses find they soon have spare time. Take it as a chance to join a book group and read those books you have always meant to, make a model plane and go fly it, or enrol in a distance learning course and do the study you had always wanted to achieve. Do anything that appeals to you, just keep busy, active and mentally stimulated.

If no-one does quilting and you used to enjoy your weekly circle with friends start one yourself. Make it a craft class or general sewing if there are few people or no-one else who quilts. Teach what you know. Half of the enjoyment of the quilting circle can be the shared friendship and caring. The new class will help provide new friends and become a place to discuss what's happening in your new town, where to buy things, what's happening, and keep you up with the gossip.

Not being able to maintain your original career is probably the most frustrating issue of all for many travelling spouses, but again a healthy, positive attitude can help address this. Have an open mind, stay flexible and don't turn down any suggestion immediately. Think it through thoroughly: try voluntary work. It can be very irksome to think that previously you were well paid and now do the same work for free, but it could keep you in contact with the field, looks good on a future CV, and helps you get back on the career track when an opportunity arises. Use it to improve yourself in areas where you are currently less skilled. Treat it as a learning experience – a non-certificate degree. Language, business skills and computer software programs are good areas for self-development. Find a charity you want to support and work for them. It is easy to see how some professions can volunteer or adapt. Doctors, nurses, physiotherapists and so on can volunteer in orphanages, old people's homes or hospitals for example. Accountants make marvellous treasurers for all sorts of clubs and societies. Computer literate people are also always welcome. However, for those of us with less obvious applications, simply speaking English can be helpful and organisational skills are needed by most groups. Voluntary work has a very strong 'feel good factor' attached to it, and you are contributing to the improvement of the society where you are a guest. But it also has many other paybacks: it is a great introduction into the society where you live; it gets you out of the house meeting new people; it broadens your skill level; and a lot of job offers are given directly, not advertised. People see you as a capable working person and offers arrive that might not have come otherwise.

For more ideas and inspiration read *A Career in Your Suitcase*, also from Summertime Publishing.

Mind their language

There are things in a different country that always end up being fears, worries or problems that prey in the back of our minds and make us unhappy. Focus on these and find a way within the place and culture you are living to address them. Language and cultural standards are one of the first and most obvious. Without a common language, even solving simple tasks becomes an emotional and mental minefield. Admittedly sign language quickly becomes refined to a high art but even just getting the language basics makes a big difference. It is not just what you say, but the fact that you, as a newcomer, are trying to learn their language and are making an effort. Locals appreciate this and you will be much better received and treated. It used to really infuriate me that our staff giggled whenever they were told off. Finally it was explained to me. Indonesians, like several other Asian groups, use laughter to cope with embarrassment. Simply understanding why it was happening made it easier to get used to. Make a point of trying to become familiar with at least the language basics and cultural norms. Using these, you can deal with many other issues that may frustrate you.

Don't get angry – sort it out

If you live in a remote area and hospitals are hard to reach don't panic about how you will cope in an emergency. City traffic jams or poor standards of health care in remote locations can be daunting, but there are ways of dealing with it. I gave up five days of holiday in Australia to do a super course run by ambulance officers. Initially I felt frustrated and resentful at having to spend the time on it, but I ended up learning a lot, enjoying the course and best of all, much more comfortable that I could cope if something happened. If it is an important issue to you, get it resolved.

and finally . . .

A new location is a new set of experiences. It is a positive challenge. After all, not everyone gets to travel and have someone else pay for it. If you use the time to learn the language, immerse yourself in the local culture or as a time to mentally develop yourself, try a new career path or do something you've been wanting to do for years but never had time for previously. Years later you too will look back on that time spent overseas with fond recollections. The underlying key is learning, understanding and accepting the new place you are in and making the most of your time.

How to Be Happy – Naturally
by
Karen Bird

Karen's career in England had been very important to her. Then she moved to the Sultanate of Oman and spent ten years on a voyage of self-discovery and creativity.

Many things have made my life happy – family and friends, work, home, hobbies and holidays, being alone, a good film, a good meal, a wedding, a birth. But until I came to Oman I didn't realise how much I relied on things outside me to feel good. What I wanted to was to feel good in me all the time, or as much as I could. And not just when I was doing special things but when I was quiet, when cooking, walking or sitting, alone. I wanted everyday things to feel special too. It seemed the only way to make sense of a world which seemed crazy at times.

In England I was part of a close family and had long-lasting friends. I had enjoyed working in the mental health field for many years, in a variety of areas ranging from children in community homes to elderly people in psychiatric hospitals. I spent some years doing therapeutic group work with young people and then moved to individual support work and counselling with adults. Work was vitally important to me and my identity.

I grew up in London and loved city life, though I needed the space and fresh air of the countryside too. With plenty of physical and mental energy I had lots of hobbies and interests in a variety of crafts. I sewed, embroidered, knitted, did pottery, photography, and dabbled with the piano and guitar. I exercised with yoga, swimming, and walking, as well as occasional karate and horse riding from time to time. I wasn't the most relaxed person – I had to work at it. There were some emotional ups and downs in my private life. I had a restless streak, I was curious, searching. I loved learning new things. I had not found life easy but on the other hand I was never bored. Life could be scary and depressing but over-all I found it interesting, sometimes exciting and, on rare occasions, pure bliss.

By my mid 30s I was living alone for the first time after the break up of my first marriage. I enjoyed the freedom of coming and going as I wished, not having to discuss what to eat or what colour to paint the walls; I loved having less of a rou-tine. I had a dog and a cat and spent a lot of time walking in Yorkshire where I then lived. I wasn't looking for another husband, not consciously that is, but I found one through a very chance meeting. Denis was working overseas and after two years of letter writing, extortionate phone bills and several visits to the Middle East where he was living, we married and I moved to Oman to be with him. Like many a self-deluded expatriate wife (I've met loads), I told myself it would be for a year or two. I saw it as a sabbatical or time out, an opportunity to review and refresh, before going back to my life at home. I got it wrong. For a start, nearly ten years on, I'm still here.

Going Down

I left England thinking I was adaptable, flexible, strong. I had always loved trav-el and new places. I came in a spirit of adventure and felt good but that didn't last long. My enthusiasm for this new life went out of the window fast. I missed the obvious things like family and friends. I missed my house and my things. I missed the stimulation and structure of work, colleagues, common interests, feeling useful, as though in some small way I was contributing to a more har-monious world. Work gave me space to air views and to discuss life; I was used to having a voice. I missed crowded streets, city parks, cinemas, concerts and galleries; the smell of earth, country walks, deep-rooted trees. I also missed bookshops and cafes – my two favourite haunts. I often felt tired and sometimes quite scared, and alternated between tears and rage. It felt quite unreal, like I'd walked on to a film set – and the wrong one at that. In short, I felt grief. Grief usu-ally describes the feelings of loss after a death and, while I didn't compare my own losses to that, I believe what I felt was similar. I could identify some of the stages of shock, denial, anger and pain, then withdrawal and finally acceptance and peace that experts often describe in their studies of loss and death.

I didn't have children, not something I noticed, so to speak, in England. I had been engrossed in a career and there had never been a 'right time'. I had nephews and nieces, godchildren I was close to, as well as friends without children. I had not felt I'd missed out. But Muscat seemed to be full of young children and I felt I neither fitted in with the younger couples who planned or had a family, nor with women a bit older than me whose children had grown up. With two recently acquired teenage stepdaughters who were at school in England and only spent holidays with us, I had no sense of a peer group. I felt lonely for the first time in my life – and guilty too. It was peaceful, safe and sunny in Oman. What more could I want? With material needs taken care of, life here offered great opportunity to seek higher things but that was a frightening experience for me then.

Help!

It was a gradual process, one step forward, two steps back. The smallest things could make or break a day – a few friendly words from someone in the supermarket, walking through the old alleys selling spices in Mutrah Souq on the plus side; while my hair going wrong or having to make polite conversation at a dinner party with a dozen people I didn't know could bring on panic and tears.

It was a love-hate thing. I didn't like where we lived. For a start the villa was single storey and I felt oppressed living on the ground floor. I had spent many years in converted loft rooms. I felt I could breathe when I lived up high. INow I was living in a suburban area with neat little streets set round a complex of shops. I'd imagined something far more exotic with my senses being overpowered by new sights, sounds, smells and tastes. I did love the light though and the winter sun; months of warm evenings outside; weekends spent camping in the desert or on near empty beaches. It never was all bad, though there were days when it felt like it was.

I felt lost. I didn't recognise myself or my life. I was frustrated at having to acknowledge what I saw as my shortcomings at not fitting in. I was lonely for the first time in my life, and furious with my husband, Oman, and myself. I felt I was waiting for something else, waiting to leave, to resume my career, to live somewhere that felt more me, for life to look up.

A typical day for me was to wake tired with a heavy feeling in my chest. I'd give myself a little pep talk to get out of bed. It seemed for years I had to pull myself up my bootstrings. At the same time I felt no-one noticed, and while on the one hand I was pleased about that, I felt quite unreal for a couple of years with the effort of being cheerful and all right. It wasn't that the people were unfriendly, more that most seemed to have their lives all set up.

It sounds churlish, but for a good two years I felt this was the last place on earth I would have chosen to be. (Never mind that I DID choose it – I'd changed my mind.) The imposing barren mountains seemed inaccessible, not easy to climb or to walk. They felt like the wall of a prison with the sea hemming me in on the other side. Many times I wanted scream. I longed for the crowds of Bombay, the traffic of Bangkok, the struggle of life in Siberia – anything that was the antithesis of Oman.

Now while I have found a way of being here that is happy and satisfying, and I believe that the place of truth is within, I still hold that there is something in the geography with which we are, as individuals, more naturally in tune. Having read books on Feng Shui, the ancient Chinese art of understanding how landscapes, buildings, room arrangements can affect your life and health, I also accept there are still places where I feel more at home. It's a personal thing – I also know many people who are happy here and don't want to leave.

Eventually I realised that nothing happens until you take the first step. 'Grasp the nettle' as my father used to say (and he made us do it as kids just to prove that something you thought would hurt didn't when you took a firm grip). There has been a constant confirmation of 'Something always turns up'. I would add 'When you're ready, when you say yes to whatever is around'. Around this time I used a selection of Bach Flower Remedies (see later) as a positive step towards inner happiness.

Once I began to accept that this was home, that 'today' was everything, that if it wasn't okay here, how could it be okay anywhere else, then things started to shift. My resistance had not helped: it had blocked me, kept me where I was. I have for years felt that it was the wanting something to be different that caused the hurt, and I became sure of this through my own experience. And in the many self-help books I have read, the message has always been clear – that it is not circumstances nor situations that make you unhappy, but what is inside you and how you deal with it. Who's to say that if you are unhappy in Warsaw you might not also be unhappy in Wisconsin or Wimbledon. It is easy to blame other people and exterior forces for the way you feel. But from the day I decided to call Muscat home and stop fighting, I was on the up.

I have had to think long and hard about what I truly want from life, from myself and from my relationships. I have explored uncharted, and often painful, territory as I have looked inside myself. I haven't always liked what I found, but the most important thing has been to discover the power of my own mind.

While the journey up my spiritual mountain has been far from smooth, the view from the top is breathtaking. What follows are my personal experiences on what has worked for me. Use them as a starting point for your own journey in pursuit of inner peace and natural happiness. Our tastes may be different. Keep an open mind, read, research, talk to people explore, experiment, expand.

Watch out for the signposts that are sure to appear. You too can find your own plateau of peace.

Go for it

Many things have helped me but some especially stand out. There have been clear turning points. It's been a challenge. I have taken jobs I would never have tried, such as teaching English and publishing. I have taken the opportunity to make friends with people I would not otherwise have met and now have friends from Iran, Poland, Holland, New Zealand, America, India, and Ireland. I have discovered new interests such as singing and snorkelling, ice skating, sculpting, and more recently playing the drums. Being here has stretched my imagination in the absence of the familiar and accepted diversions such as entertainment and educational or special interest courses I could have taken in England. I often found unexpected support in new friends, and an inner discipline to explore and help myself that I didn't know I had.

I have used many natural therapies and self-help techniques. New paths have constantly emerged and there has been much to guide and uplift me. I now have good friends in like-minded people, some of whom I met through a wonderfully creative group of people who meet regularly to disucss alternative therapies, food and diet and self-help techniques. As well as that, I have read many books on self-discovery and I've written enough journals to make several books.

Home and Away

Going home twice a year has been essential for me to keep my life going there. Family relationships and close friendships, rather than diminishing, have grown as we make the most of the time we have together. I've always made the time to be with friends when I've gone home. I haven't rushed from pillar to post, but have usually preferred to spend two or three days with fewer people. Letting go of some friends can be painful and upsetting, but travelling miles for brief conversations is tiring and unsatisfying all round. Being 4000 miles away concentrates the mind and it has certainly been easier to appreciate what is most precious in life.

After many painful leavings when I'd cry as the plane took off, I said 'enough'. I'd had it with sadness – I wanted to feel good. One day I decided to start looking forward to coming back here. In the days leading up to departure I would consciously take off my rose-coloured spectacles and count my blessings instead. I would concentrate hard on the clear skies and azure seas, majestic sand dunes and vast red deserts, my husband Denis playing his saxophone and old tribal rugs on the marble floors. Now I no longer feel that separation, and, instead, feel both connected and released.

I have also used home leaves to catch up on those courses and have studied writing, editing, photography, massage, Reiki (a natural healing technique) and more. This has helped provide stimulation and increased skills as well as giving me the chance to meet people of like mind.

Working It Out

When I arrived in Muscat, newly married and with a suitcase full of false perceptions, not least about my own needs, the most natural first thing to do was to find work. I started out volunteering once a week at the thrift shop in the local church which gave me a small amount of structure, something to do and a way of meeting people. A four week intensive TEFL course (Teacher of English as a Foreign Language) turned out to serve me well for three years. I started out teaching English to children, then to the South American wives of Denis' colleagues, which helped us all to fit in. I went on to work in one of the local adult schools and enjoyed meeting Omani people who were warm and friendly as well as generally eager to learn.

I always liked writing and had spent many hours on letters home about my life here. As a child I would tell my sister and brother stories in bed, and wrote the beginnings of stories as well poetry and prose. Writing seemed one of the few things that it really made sense to do by correspondence, and in a burst of inspiration and energy I went into the The London School of Journalism and signed for a freelance journalism course. Through it I gained the confidence to contact editors in Muscat and Dubai about freelance work. Only a year later I was offered a job in a local publishing company.

For two and a half years I earned money from writing, researching news stories and articles. I learned to proof read, and took photographs too. I was enjoying opportunities I had only previously dreamed of. I met the Russian State Ballet and local artists and went to Sri Lanka and Jordan to do travel features. I reviewed hotels and restaurants and met people who have become good friends. I learned a lot, not least about myself. It was an exercise in transferring skills I could use my people skills and was good at PR. But I was still new to much of it, and gradually younger and more experienced people came in.

With little chance to develop myself further it became time to move on but I panicked at the thought of not having a job. I thought I'd procrastinate without the routine and social side of work, and I'd have no income of my own. Maybe I was more than a little scared of being alone with my thoughts? After much soul searching, though, I took a chance and resigned. Having never allowed myself to be idle before, I felt guilty and in limbo again. But then a strange thing happened. Call it fate if you like, or 'synchronicity'. Within a few months I was offered a part time job in a second hand bookshop. I was also asked to do various writing and editing jobs. Over the next three years I worked freelance on a gardening book, company and hotel newsletters, and a travel guide on Oman. Despite my resolve I was still working.

Hands On

I started out seeing creativity in a narrow way. I thought it was just about painting pictures or writing books. I also thought that I truly wanted to be a writer. After
my voyage of self-discovery I ended up with a far broader feeling of what creativity was about and a craving to use my hands. About this time, I dragged
myself to an exhibition to support a friend and in the true synchronistic fashion,
I was introduced to a woman called Sally Ricketts who had not long arrived.
Sally was a sculptor with both kiln and clay. She didn't give lessons but liked
people working alongside her at her home.

Sally uses a variety of clays to make full size portrait heads. With a fascina-
tion for traditional costume of Oman, she has incorporated the colourful and
ornate dress into figures of women and children, and men as well. Her abun-
dantly green garden, where we work in the winter months, also contains bird
houses and huge planters in the shape of strange faces on the house walls. My
time at Sally's has been wonderful. Small groups of people meet there every day
of the week. Sally provides a great ambience and opportunity to explore yourself
freely without any demands. We use no wheels, only hands. I have taken up
sculpting which I discovered I love, and my husband's head now sits in our hall-
way along with small abstract figures, candle holders and burners for essential
oils as well as vases and bowls.

Yet while I pondered about my long term ambitions I kept returning to the idea
that aromatherapy massage could well be an ideal career option. I had used
essential oils for 12 years or so, in the bath and in burners around the house. I'd
had massage and had found it relaxing and stabilising in times of stress. I loved
the smells of the oils and, with increasingly good immunity, I realised their therapeutic value too. It was at this time that I met astrologer Maggy van Krimpen at
the Writers Circle. She specialised in guidance on careers. At my reading she
told me to use my hands. This gave me faith in my own inclinations and I went
on to enrol with an aromatherapy school in London that ran a course for students
overseas.

Then I heard of the ancient healing technigue of Reiki (see later) through
Valerie Lee, the reflexologist I was going to. She'd just done a course with a visiting Reiki Master/Teacher who was planning a return visit. I didn't understand
much about it and was mildly curious. But just before the teacher arrived I suddenly felt a strong interest and a clear certainty that it was for me. After the first
course I had a very happy year indeed. This led me to be certain that I should
take the second level when I was next in England. This time the result was completely different and very unexpected. Although at the end of the weekend
course I had a sense of being in the right place in myself, six weeks later back
in Oman, I became very tired. Low moods alternated with anger in the following
few months, and things I felt I had long sorted out raised their heads. It seemed
everything in my life was up for review: friends, marriage, home, work, my

behaviour, my whole lifestyle in fact. Situations became frustrating, things stopped working as smoothly as they had, and I noticed people often cancelled arrangements with me at the last minute. I carried on working at the two jobs I had editing a newsletter and working in the secondhand bookshop. At first, I was convinced my changing hormones were causing this havoc, but my friend in England who did the course with me was also feeling unsettled. We discovered that we felt similar with stages of ill health, tiredness; we were upset and angry, not wanting to do the things we usually did, with a sense of going into retreat. I was even more convinced that when things outside appear not to be working then there's only one place to go — within. The effect of the Reiki was that I at last began to surrender to my instinct and relax. A calm was descending. I believed I was taking it easy at last — but I was still working.

On the Up

Then, a year ago, nine years into my decade in Muscat, we moved house. I had wanted to move for a while to something that felt more like mine. It was time. In an idle moment, daydreaming, I wrote down all I wanted — a private room in which to work, balconies with a sea view, a patio garden with bushes and trees and wooden units in a kitchen large enough to have a table at which we could eat there. I wanted to walk to restaurants, the shops, and the sea. I put the list away out of sight and, unusually for me, out of mind. We gave notice to our landlord, yet had nowhere to go.

I occasionally drove around the area I liked but saw nothing to rent. A few weeks before we were due to move out I drove past the road where we now live and felt a definite pull in my chest. An inner voice told me that my house was there and to be patient. A few days later I looked in the paper, saw a house to rent (there had been very few) and viewed it the next day. It was my house in every detail. It was in exactly the road where I felt it would be. In ten days we had the keys and we moved in after three weeks. I attribute this bit of magic to a combination of the law of attraction at work, being absolutely clear of what I wanted while at the same time letting it go. I knew that if I had tried to force the hand of fate it could block the natural chain of events.

With the keys in early May and the house still being repainted, we took fold-up chairs, sundowners and snacks and spent a week of evenings on the roof of the empty house, looking out to the sea. We could smell the perfume of unidentified flowers, and flocks of parrots flew over our heads as the sun set in the trees. With a small shopping centre just across the road, some restaurants, and a large car park next to the beach, it may not sound so alluring to everyone, but to me, the sound of cars and seeing people walking around, were just bliss. And it so happened that for our first two evenings on the roof there were dramatic lightening storms, but no rain, which we sat watching for hours, entranced. We both love storms, a rare occurrence here, and we took it as a welcome and felt very glad.

The day we moved in was when my shoulder seized up. I couldn't sleep that first night for the pain. I wandered around the house and at 3am in the kitchen. And it was there that I noticed a kind of gentle breath move through the ground floor like a wave. My husband said the next day it was a sigh of relief.

But the pain in my shoulder did not go away and still felt tired. I began meditating daily with a tape by a Buddhist called Maitreya who has a Japanese garden and meditation centre near where I live in England. His voice is comforting and powerful. The feeling of wanting to retreat was important and I could have taken more notice than I did. In fact, I am sure it's because I ignored that feeling earlier that my shoulder seized up to tell me to stop. Even then I couldn't and kept on working though I could neither drive nor write. But eventually I got the message and when I finally stopped working altogether the pain and tiredness eased. This, for me, was the final and vital step. I let go at last.

Now I lived by the beach I used it – never mind that it was 100° F outside. For the first time I did not mind the heat and walked every day which seemed to help. I felt more peaceful – if sweaty – and in the right place. I began using Reiki again too and by the time I went home in August I felt much more healthy and relaxed.

Eight weeks in England restored me as always. I spent time with family and friends and got a good dose of London air. I came back to Oman truly resolved not to take any work at all – a complete breakthrough for me as I'd always worked, my biggest fear being losing a professional identity. But I felt stronger, clearer in my mind than I'd been for a long time, with different ideas forming about what was important in life. Peace of mind was becoming a priority, which meant understanding and letting go of the thoughts that prevented this. A line from Marianne Williamson's book *A Return to Love On a Course in Miracles* comes to mind: ' Do you prefer to be right or happy?'

Going On

I am much more relaxed now and I know how to take the best care of myself. I know what I want, when I want it – I listen in to and trust in myself. I am beginning to realise the power of my mind and the unlimited creative potential we all have. I enjoy my own company and spend more time alone, while friendships are closer and my marriage is good. Doing the last level of Reiki training in April 1998 has brought a feeling of a circle joined and a greater peace. Opportunities to do things I like keep turning up.

I'm getting better at noticing what I call first thoughts the gut ones that often get silenced by our old friend the censor. Practising acting on them though is a great lesson in self trust, and I waste less energy wondering, storing things up.

At last, I procrastinate less. My closest friends feel the change Margaret said I looked different and very happy and Ewa said 'You have stopped!' Denis finds me lovely to live with and allows me to be who I am.

As I sit here in on my balcony listening to the lilting call to prayer and with the smell of Jasmine and Frangipani hanging thickly on the evening air, I feel at peace. I no longer feel like I'm in a waiting room – a journey yes, never ending, ongoing, and I am open to whatever comes next. I can see more clearly and at the same time nothing matters but the present. I have no work and less interest in that than ever before. I have stopped longing for things I don't have and no longer feel the loss of the longing. I am not constantly planning for the future. I feel at this moment in connection with my true inner self and the source of all life. Things are going well. There's an ease. I am learning how to be. And being is happy – naturally.

Karen would like to share details of the following natural therapies with you :

Aromatherapy and Massage

Aromatherapy is an holistic therapy that takes account of the whole person and his or her lifestyle. It uses essential oils distilled from plants to treat a whole range of physical and emotional problems as diverse as, for example, tiredness and stress, stiff muscles, cystitis and high blood pressure. A qualified therapist will make up your individual blend based on assessment of your physical and emotional state at the time. The oils must be diluted in a vegetable carrier oil, and are most powerfully used in massage to combine a hands on treatment that leaves most people feeling, at the very least, wonderfully relaxed. It is also a fast and enjoyable way of getting the therapeutic properties of the oils into the body. Regular massage with essential oils stimulates the body's own defence mechanisms and brings about balance, so it is a good preventive technique. With or without using oils, massage has a powerful effect on general health, by improving circulation and digestion, and stimulating the lymphatic system. It helps release emotional as well as muscular tension, and is a great way to feel comforted and looked after. Massage brings relaxation and balance at all levels – body, mind and spirit too.

Massage has helped me in stressful times at work, backache, tiredness, and during the months when my first marriage broke up, it helped keep me sane.

The benefits of massage are cumulative. When I was doing the intensive practical part of my aromatherapy course, we all gave and received a full body massage every day for eight days. By day seven I felt I was about to levitate off the couch under the hands of my Latvian co–student, and took hold of the sides just in case. By the end of the course I felt so open and filled with a sense of well–being, that as I made my way across London back to my parents, I found myself touching complete strangers in the street who asked me for directions. I must have looked like a walking A–Z so many people approached me

Reflexology
The origins of reflexology go back thousands of years. It is both a diagnostic tool and a treatment in itself. Like acupuncture and shiatsu, reflexology works with the lines of meridian energy flowing through the body, on which traditional Chinese medicine is based. The therapist presses on specific points, usually with the thumbs, which link with a network of nerves connected to all the organs and muscles of the body. Through this she can identify areas of tension, blocks in energy and specific problems. The treatment helps clear away blocks, encourages circulation, and generally helps restore balance, vitality and therefore, health, to the body. Reflexology feels wonderful. At the very least, like massage, it is relaxing. After my first session I could hardly stand up. I made the mistake of stopping off at the supermarket and when I tried to speak to someone I knew, my speech was so slurred she must have thought I was drunk. I felt wonderful the next day, however. I found reflexology very comforting as a treatment but much of that was as much to do with the therapist, Valerie Lee. She provided a secure ambience, with soft lighting, relaxing music and candles, as well as a most comfortable chair. She was very peaceful to be with and after the initial consultation, she worked quietly, often with her eyes closed, but gave me her full attention when I talked and in the first few sessions I found myself offloading a lot of what was on my mind. It was a great release emotionally and helped me relax and feel cared for.

Bach Remedies
These simple flower essences are a great way of helping yourself and in my first few years here I relied on Bach Remedies a lot. Discovered by a doctor and biologist Edward Bach in the 1930s, the remedies are based on his belief that happiness is a natural state of being, and that unhappiness is the cause of ill–health. The 38 remedies treat states of mind rather than symptoms and like other natural therapies they stimulate and balance the body's own resources. They are safe and simple to use, fine for children, animals and even for plants. There are people qualified to advise you on which to choose and you can visit the Dr Bach Centre at the cottage where he lived in England for a consultation. When I visited some years ago, I sat quietly in Dr Bach's peaceful room on the same wood chairs he made for himself, overlooking the garden, where the remedies are still produced in the same way.

My experience of Bach remedies is that they deal with things in layers, as and when you are ready to do so. I'd take remedies like Walnut for protection in times of change, Scleranthus for indecision, White Chestnut for unwanted thoughts, two drops in water or four under the tongue – for a couple of weeks. Then I'd forget to take them, which was a sign to me that I no longer needed them. The change would be subtle, I'd suddenly realise I felt better. Maybe weeks or months later another part of me would present itself. These days I don't think to take them but I always keep a bottle of Rescue Remedy in the house, a combination of five remedies for shock or short term stress.

Astrology

I enjoyed the only astrological reading I've ever had. I'd had mixed feelings about the whole subject, what with horoscopes in the dailies, though I felt sure we must be influenced by the universe out there. When I was thinking about ways of working in the future, I met Maggy van Krimpen, an astrologer with a special interest in career guidance. I gave her my details over the phone date, time and place of birth – and a few weeks later I went to her house where she interpreted my chart. Analysing the three main areas of planetary arrangement at the time of my birth Maggy talked about the various aspects of my personality and how conflicts can arise when these are not fully understood.

Maggy talked as though she was an old friend who knew me very well which of course she didn't before working on my chart. She helped clarify some contradictions and the potential difficulties these can cause, as well as giving me guidance on how to enhance innate abilities and skills. She highlighted some specific events in my life, and got close to their dates, which I found disconcerting, as though I could not have avoided some things that had happened to me, but she explained it was just that I was vulnerable to that kind of thing.

She spoke of how important it has been for me to use my intellect, which I agreed with – but that stronger in my chart was a more primitive person who must use her hands. She suggested aromatherapy to start with, which I'd been considering, but said I'd go on to do other things with my hands, and I have what with Reiki, sculpting, bio–energy – and when I do these things I feel in tune with myself. Listening again to the tape of my reading in order to write this, I am reminded of Maggy saying I have a lot of physical energy that I often don't make the most of and how I need to make more of a noise. In the past year I have been craving to dance – which I do in privacy at home – and more recently drumming has helped me feel more balanced and on track.

Counselling and Psychotherapy

Some brief psychotherapy in London helped clear my mind a couple of years after I came to Oman. I was feeling bogged down, couldn't think straight and knew I needed someone outside of this situation to help me make sense of it. The therapist at the Group Analytic Practice was not your blank screen, Freudian type, but challenged the way I was thinking and offered practical suggestions as to how I could look at my situation differently and take more responsibility for myself. For example, she directed me to an organisation called International Social Services and although I got nowhere with that, it was good to meet with people in London and start thinking about other things I could do. Three sessions of counselling with a psychologist here two years ago similarly helped when I wanted to talk over some of the changes I was going through with an objective professional. Friends are good to talk to and I have always done that too, but there are times when you need someone uninvolved with you who can see things in a fresh and clear way, who will challenge what you say and not let you kid yourself – not always easy for friends.

Meditation and Visualisation
There are many ways to meditate in order to quieten the mind you, to get closer to your real self, to reach a different place of consciousness, a happier state of being. During meditation the brain slows down to alpha waves, and the heart and metabolism slow down as well, which produces a relaxed but alert state. Methods include breath counting or repeating a mantra, focussing on a flower or candle flame. Having used various techniques over the last 25 years and not had much success with the sitting cross–legged, counting breaths kind, I prefer more active visualisations where you imagine or see things in your mind to work on. I have used visualisation – or imagework as Dina Glouberman calls it in her excellent book *Life Choices and Life Changes Through Imagework* – for getting guidance on how to do something such as write this, for improving my health or relationships, for understanding what I really want, for solving problems, for renewing energy and more.
As well as all this, I often feel in a meditative state when I do pottery and sculpting, when I walk alone on the beach, when I dance or sing, when I daydream, and sometimes when I drum. Meditation for me is anything that brings us into the moment, to a quieter place deep inside, when the everyday world with its worries goes away and there's contentment instead.

Osteopathy
I gradually became more interested in the mind–body link. The more I read and took note of my physical feelings and discomforts the more they made sense as messages and opportunities to change something instead. A long-term back problem recurred when I first came to Oman. I assumed it was stress. It came on after flying, sitting at the computer for a long time or after I'd been upset. With more time and opportunity to explore other avenues I went to Katia Twyford, an osteopath here who applied a cranial-sacral tecnique.
As well as working on my physical body using various movements, less dramatic and more gentle than osteopathy often is – she seemed able to tune into more subtle energies and used visualisation and symbols as well to help me get in touch with emotional issues which were creating physical blocks. During treatment the therapist feels the pulse of cerebrospinal fluid, in the brain and spine, which gives information about the body, and is effective with many bodily conditions.
I became conscious in the first couple of sessions that my head had never felt

comfortable on my neck, as though it was too heavy and not straight. After six sessions over some months I was surprised to find my head and neck feeling aligned. I remember walking along the beach after my last session feeling strong, straight and light. It felt great. Now my back gives me few problems, and when it occasionally does I say thank you for the reminder that I need to stop.

Reiki
It is thought that Reiki originated in Tibet but it was rediscovered by Dr Mikao Usui in the mid 1800s and brought to Japan. This ancient healing technique uses natural energy to balance the whole being by placing the hands on various points of the body. It works at all levels – physical, mental, emotional and spiritual – to bring harmony and health. Reiki also seems to be a catalyst for increasing awareness of the spiritual self and brings about inevitable change. The Reiki philosophy is simply to not anger or worry just for today, to honour parents, teachers and elders, to earn your living honestly, to bless what you have and be kind to every living thing.

Each level of training takes two to four days of theory and practice, with what are known as attunements a ritual specific to Reiki training, to open or attune you to the energy of Reiki. There are no tests or exams, and it is up to each person to use Reiki after the attunements to develop it for themselves. First degree Reiki is primarily for self-healing, while Reiki 2 enables you to send the energy over time and space for distance healing and the third and last level is that of Reiki master and teacher.

Both giving and receiving Reiki is a relaxing and enjoyable experience. The person receiving lies on a couch fully clothed, while the person or persons giving it place their hands on various of positions on the body for a few minutes in each place. It can be comforting and relaxing both to give and receive. Gentle music often plays in the background and usually the session is carried out quietly. The hands of the giver often become warm, which the receiver can usually feel, and hands may tingle, especially around problem areas.

Bio-energy
A visiting therapist from Ireland, Patricia Rafferty, introduced bio-energy here a few years ago. Bio-energy is a great mix of science and mysticism, as well as a powerful healing tool that has had some amazing results. Patricia uses this practical healing technique to work on the energy field or aura surrounding the body. The theory behind bio-energy is that past trauma, accidents, surgery or distress, whether physical or emotional, are held in the energy field. Healing of this can happen spontaneously as the person takes care of his or herself, but often it seems that a memory of the hurt remains until it is released and healed by someone like Patricia who has the ability, sensitivity and skill to feel, and often see, the human energy field.

I had a course of treatment myself when Patricia first came, more out of curiosity than anything else, but she picked up an old upset which she worked on in four sessions of half an hour on consecutive days. These induced a feeling of comfort and safety after which I felt happier and physically and emotionally more at ease. Patricia works close to the body, using her hands to feel out any irregularities in the energy field, and swirling them around in circles as she removed any blocks. Sometimes I felt warm, sometimes cold, and my body swayed back and forth at times. Then she places her hands on points of the body such as shoulder and hip to bring further balance.

Music
Music has always played a large part in my life and I have appreciated that even more here.

I have sung in a choir and have entertained friends who play various instruments and sing, and I now take drum lessons, though I have no aspirations to be in a rock band. As well as being a great stress reliever, drumming gives me a satisfaction that is hard to describe. I am hooked – the more I do the more I want to do. I read an article recently about how drumming synchronises the left and right hemispheres of the brain, and another on how in America Mickey Hart of Grateful Dead fame has been working with the healing and therapeutic effects of playing drums.

Writing with a Difference
Wanting to explore writing further I went on a workshop called Write to Life in London in 1994, run by Nigel Watts, an author of four books. The course encouraged us to put the editor or inner critic aside, initially by giving it a name and a form and banishing it to the other side of the room. We did group exercises to encourage communication and trust, meditated, walked, wrote short timed pieces and read them out without comment from others.

This workshop brought together a diverse group of men and women aged from 20s–50s, from a lawyer to a trapeze artist, as well as several aspiring and published writers. By the close of the weekend we inevitably felt close and I still meet up with the woman I paired up with for the last exercise.

Write to Life was based on the work of an American writer and teacher, Natalie Goldberg, who applies her Zen and Buddhist principles to writing. Back in Muscat and with a new enthusiasm I joined the Writers Circle and suddenly found an outlet for self expression that gave me confidence and strength. The other members were a mixture of people who just liked to write as well as those who had had short stories, poems and articles published. Putting my inner critic, aside I began to enjoy reading out what I'd written and having a voice. I was less interested in being published than in the feeling of trust in the group and an awe at the creativity that poured forth. I wrote most days and began to feel freer than I had done for a while as I explored myself and experimented with a new me through the words.

Then my yoga teacher and friend, A New Zealander called Andrea, showed me a book she thought I'd be interested in – *The Artist's Way*, by Julia Cameron. This book is set out as a twelve week self-study course in discovering and recovering creativity, as Cameron puts it, with a spiritual bent; it's a course in self–nurturing and self–trust. Exercises asked me to remember childhood things Id liked, explore imaginary lives, look at who and what supported me best, and I found I rather liked being my own counsellor. Once I'd started I could not put the book down. I worked on it religiously every week – the reading, the exercises and the mainstay of the course – what Cameron calls *morning pages* .

Morning pages are three pages of writing without stopping, without thinking. You just keep the pen moving and write out all immediate junk in your mind. Writing quickly gives the inner critic, your own censor, less time to get a hold. It helps you move away from left brain activity of logic and intellect, away from ego thinking, and gets you more into creative right brain stuff, – and hence closer to your less conscious self, a self that seems wiser, more interesting, nearer the spirit of your truer self.

I loved morning pages. I wrote them with great ease and still do, though their content has changed. In the early days my notebooks were full of negatives, moans and complaints about how I felt, people, lack of things missed. I also found myself writing about painful events from my distant past that I had never explored. That was not so easy. For days, maybe weeks, I'd have the feeling someone was looking over my shoulder but I braved it, got past the fear of putting things into words and breathed a sigh of relief.

Over the next three months I realised there was a change. I complained less, I saw my surroundings more positively; I'd be driving along, for example, and I'd suddenly look at the trees lining the highway or the light on the mountains and feel thankful. After about three pages it was as if my sub-conscious took over and the magic began. Snippets of stories, paragraphs, people with names I didn't know would unexpectedly appear on the page, written by me but not consciously. These days my pages contain almost no negatives, but explore ideas, ways of being, new thoughts. After a few pages my writing can change, it slows down and becomes smaller. I feel relaxed and words come but I don't know what they will be. Sometimes a kind of poetry appears, to inspire me, encourage me, clear messages of how to be.

The Artist's Way is about creativity in the widest, wildest sense. It is about finding your authentic self and being true to that whether its working at what you enjoy, cooking a meal, cleaning the house, painting a picture or growing plants. Cameron urges kindness in doing so. Through this course I became more aware of what makes me tick and became a best friend to myself.

Cameron talks too about synchronicity – Carl Jung's term for a seemingly positive order in events. Cameron says when what we get what we ask for it's easier to call it coincidence or luck, rather than admit maybe something intelligent and responsive is at work in the universe. But it is true that once you make a commitment, no matter how small, wonderful things start to happen that seem a lot more than luck.

Books and tapes

Creative Visualisation
Shakti Gawain
Bantam New Age
ISBN 0–553–27044–3

Life Choices and Life Changes through Imagework
Dina Glouberman
Mandala
ISBN 0–04–440483–2

Wild Mind
Natalie Goldberg
Rider
ISBN 0–7126–5106–3

The Artists Way
Julia Cameron
Pan Macmillan
ISBN 0330343580

A Course in Miracles Foundation for Inner Peace
Penguin
ISBN 0–670–86975–9

Anatomy of the Spirit
Caroline Myss
Bantam
ISBN 0–553–50527–0

Aromatherapy – For Healing the Spirit
Gabriel Mojay
Gaia
ISBN 1–85675–072–8

The Everyday Meditator – a practical guide
Osho
Newleaf
ISBN 0–7522–0550–1

Tapes

Complete Relaxation and Meditation
Buddha Maitreya
Available from Pureland, North Clifton, Nr Newark, Notts NG23 7AT, UK
Tel + (0)1777 228567

The Abraham Tapes
Abraham-Hicks Publications, PO Box 690070, San Antonio, TX 78269, US
Tel + 1 830 755 2299
Fax +1 830 755 4179
http://www.abraham-hicks.com
Email abraham@txdirect.net

Other useful books

Mind to Mind
Betty Shine
Corgi
ISBN 0–552–13378–7

Hands of Light
Barbara Ann Brennan
Bantam New Age
ISBN 0553345397

Light Emerging
Barbara Ann Brennan
Bantam New Age
ISBN 0–553–35456–6

Writing Down the Bones
Natalie Goldberg
Shambala
ISBN 0–87773–375–9

Feel the Fear and Do It Anyway
Susan Jeffers
Arrow
ISBN 0–09–974100–8

Mind and Movement
Tony Crisp
Daniel
ISBN 0–85207–182–5

Passage to Power
Leslie Kenton
Century Vermilion
ISBN 0091815940

Creating Sacred Space with Feng Shui
Karen Kingston
Piatkus
ISBN 0–7499–1601–x

A Return to Love
Marianne Williamson
Thorsons
ISBN 0–7225–3299–7

Chi Kung
James MacRitchie
Element
ISBN 1–86204–064–8

Shamanism – as a Spiritual Practice for Daily Life
Tom Cowan
The Crossing Press
ISBN 0–89594–838–9

Soul Retrieval
Sandra Ingerman
Harper Collins
ISBN 0062504061

Welcome Home
Sandra Ingerman
Harper San Francisco
ISBN 0–06–250267–0

Conversations with God
Neale Donald Walsch
Hodder & Stoughton
ISBN 0–340–69325–8

The Well of Creativity Interviews
Michael Toms
New Dimensions
ISBN 1–56170–375–3

Simple Abundance
Sarah Ban Breathnach
Bantam
ISBN 0–553–50662–5

Being Happy!
Andrew Matthews
Media Masters
ISBN 981–00–0664–0

There are many good books available on Reiki, aromatherapy, refelexology, and Bach Remedies.

Bach Remedies are available in most pharmacies and health food shops.

The Dr Edward Bach Healing Centre
Mount Vernon
Sotwell
Wallingford
Oxon

The London School of Journalism
37 Uxbridge Street
Hillgate Village
London
W8 7TQ

Why We Have to Laugh
by
Elizabeth Douet

Elizabeth is an American journalist and workshop presenter, married to a Frenchman. She has lived in France, Norway and Germany and specialises in research and careers .

While so many of the topics covered in the second half of this book – everything from packing to selling off belongings before a new posting – are treated lightly, most expatriates have found life on a continual moving tread mill to be very trying. Many feel more like crying than laughing when the moving company delays their shipment. Others can feel total despair at trying to mail a simple letter when uncertain of the price of postage, or even how to ask the cost of a stamp in a foreign language. Simple tasks can take on monumental proportions when expatriates find themselves placed in unfamiliar surroundings.

While a laugh won't get furniture to arrive any sooner or a letter magically mailed, laughing can be an excellent coping mechanism that helps view difficult situations in a more positive light. Robert Holden, in *Laughter, The Best Medicine*, reveals that 'laughter is accepting.' He explains that 'when we are laughing we delight in non-perfect moments in a non-ideal world.'

Any expatriate can surely attest to the fact that life is less than ideal in the early stages of a new posting. By looking at Holden's theory, then the non-perfect moments involved with shifting home and family to far-away destinations and cultures certainly offer the potential for humor.

The problem is in learning how to find humor in otherwise humorless situations. According to Holden, this is a matter of perspective and something that can be changed, with constant practice of course. 'By laughing at events of life, instead of running away, for instance, we do see things differently. When we see differently, we feel differently and we behave differently,' Holden states.

If moving were viewed as a continual growth opportunity rather than a threat, then maybe all the mishaps involved juggling family, work and personal values in a foreign environment could be less intense. Holden would perhaps be the first to admit that this shift in perspective would take an enormous amount of practise. With a well-developed sense of humor, however, expatriates might be less likely to get stuck on the hurdles which all too often accompany living abroad.

A lighter attitude may also go a long way to improving health. 'More and more, humor is being recognized as a powerful force for maintaining good mental and physical health,' according to Greg Beaubein in an article published in *Psychology*. Beaubein goes on to tell that laughter has been found to boost the immune system, helping to fight off viruses.

The first year in a new posting usually reactivates long lost aches and pains, sometimes even resulting in a chronic fatigue that just can't be beaten. It isn't uncommon for alternative healing methods – such as acupuncture, foot massage or aromatherapy –– to be highly recommended within an expatriate community in order to try and overcome a plethora of ailments.

In addition to Western medicine and alternative healing methods, it seems that having a good laugh with friends may be just as important as eating right, getting enough sleep and exercising regularly. Expatriates could benefit by having a traveling 'medicine' cabinet full of funny films, books, photos or games. A personal journal full of funny situations that cropped up when cultures crossed may be beneficial in two ways. First, by providing a memorable laugh and second by showing the writer that no matter how terrible a current cultural gaff seems, it is possible to see humor with a bit of hindsight.

Laughter can also be a gauge to determine if someone is coping. While psychologists and mental health professionals remain reserved in their use of humor in the therapy room, many have expressed that an inability to laugh at even minor upsets often signals the need for professional help. One American psychologist working with expatriates in Europe explained that 'while laughter and a positive attitude are important, people who are depressed, lonely or desperate find their pain and stress too overwhelming to laugh at anything.' Once at this critical stage, a person is more likely to see humor as a sort of mockery rather than a way to alleviate pressure.

Wendy Hanson, an American clinical psychologist, with 14 years of clinical psychology practice in Norway, has found that support groups are a very valuable coping mechanism. They offer the opportunity for participants to open up and share problems within a trusting environment. Her experience has also shown that before people can get to laughter, they often need to first experience the pain and grief associated with stressful situations. For expatriates, this usually involves saying goodbye to family, friends, old homes and old routines. Unfortunately, this step is all too often given little importance.

Throughout this book we have asked expatriates from all over the world and from a wide variety of backgrounds to share their humorous stories. While perhaps not every account has left you doubled over with laughter, we hope that you have been able to identify with a few comical situations. As the benefits of laughter and of sharing problems become more apparent for both physical and mental health, we encourage you to write down your own humorous tales and start a "funny family" journal that can travel with you. While this journal may not get your furniture to arrive on time or a letter mailed overseas either, it could provide a much-deserved laughter break while sitting on moving cartons or waiting in an endless line at the post office.

Elizabeth would like to share the following with you :

Laughter the Best Medicine
Robert Holden
Thorsons
ISBN 0722528272

Ten Tips for a Smooth Flight
by
Joanna Parfitt

Joanna is a writer, presenter and publisher who lived for ten years in Dubai, Muscat and Stavanger. She specialises in effective expatriate living, networking and portable careers.

Being *forced to fly* can bring out the best in you. The anticipation of doing something strange and new for the first time is usually far worse than taking that first step. By all means think about your move in advance, but try not to worry about it. Think positively and constructively. If you discover a problem area, try to solve it, or at least find out as much as you can. Take that first step. Be proactive. Be positive. Go for it. As Julia Cameron says in her inspiring workbook *The Artist's Way:*

'Leap and the net will appear'

After ten years on the move myself, it made sense to put together my own ten favourite tips for a smooth flight. These tips are endorsed elsewhere in this book, and will undoubtedly help you to fly.

• **Tip No 1 – Research Before You Go**

Evidence suggests that going to a new posting in a positive frame of mind affects your stay considerably. If you have no idea what to expect, then, chances are, you will not be feeling very positive. You may, for example, be certain that there will be no international school for your children, no photography class for you and no chance of buying Bran Flakes. All these negative thoughts will make you dread your new assignment. But worrying won't get you anywhere and assuming the worst never helps. So try to find out before you go. Even as I write Arthur Andersen together with Craighead Publications and the Economic Intelligence Unit are setting up CountryNet™, an Internet based location research resource.

The Federation of American Women's Clubs Overseas has 15,000 members worldwide who would love to help you settle in. Check whether your company is setting up web pages or can provide printed resources for each location. The Culture Shock! series of books published by Times Publications has produced books on many countries. Resident Abroad magazine puts together a Survival Kit or useful information to help ease your transition. Topics include arriving overseas, culture shock, education, pension planning, UK taxation, banking and employment packages.

It's a good idea to talk to people who have either lived in, or know someone who has lived in, the country you are moving to. Call the British Council Information Centre and ask them if they have an office or library in your new country. Unless you happen to be the first non-local person to set foot in your new location, there is bound to be a way that you can talk to someone in the know. So, if you find out that, indeed, they do not sell Marmite in Bogota, you can be prepared and take some with you.

Remember: The more informed you are, the more positive you will become and the better your chance of a contented life.

- ## Tip No 2 – Be Proactive

Proactivity is just that, doing something about it. Its opposite, 'reactivity', is moaning about it, blaming others or situations but without seeing the solutions.

When I lived in Stavanger, Norway, I often used to walk round a lake for exercise. Surrounded by beautiful and inspiring scenery, it was the perfect place to think. Sometimes I would walk with my friend Alice Hurley, who for me has long been a positive outlook role model. It was on one of these walks on a crisp autumn day, when the silver birch trees were aflame, that she described proactivity in a way that really worked for me.

'If you don't like something you are doing you can either change it, accept it or leave it – but don't moan about it.'

One way to counteract the reactivity that we all can be prey to is to surround yourself with proactive people. We all have problems and down times and it is easy to kid ourselves that it is comforting to sit down with a cup of coffee and a relative stranger and have a good grumble. But one gripe leads to another and before long you are even more depressed than before. When you are being reactive things do not get better.

So choose your friends from among the cheerful faces you meet along the way. It may be pouring with rain for the tenth day in a row, but, as Katherine Prendergast says so poignantly 'Proactive people take their weather with them.' Look for the person whose countenance is not as grey as the leaden sky, and introduce yourself.

- ## Tip No 3 – Build a Support Team

As an expatriate, you are automatically away from familiar surroundings, family and friends.

A support team is made up of the people you can rely on. When you are constantly on the move you have to make friends quickly. Often it can be invaluable to have a soulmate, and you can help yourself to find one. If you are a keen writer, as I am, then join or start an informal writers' group. That way you will find yourself talking to people who think like you do and appreciate the same things. People who speak the same language can be a comfort.

Find someone you can rely on in times of need. When there is a crisis you can be sure that far more people will offer help than you expected. If you make friends with people who have children of similar ages to your own, then sleepovers can help compensate for not being able to leave children with grandparents.

Try to find the names of a reliable doctor, dentist, car mechanic or electrician early on. Otherwise you could find yourself flat on the floor with your finger over a burst pipe, unable to waste time battling with a foreign telephone operator as you try to find an emergency plumber. Keep the list of phone numbers by the telephone and relax in the knowledge that you are prepared for a crisis.

- ## Tip No 4 – Keep in Touch

Sometimes your support team can be made up of people who live in another country. Women like to talk. When a woman has a problem she often prefers not to bottle it up and the very act of sharing her feelings can help her feel better. To have someone who understands you well on the end of a telephone can be a great comfort, if expensive. But you don't necessarily need a phone to keep in touch.

During the ten years I was abroad my mother and I wrote to each other religiously every Sunday. The letters were little more than diaries, detailing the trivial and not so trivial events of the previous week. We both derived great comfort from these over the years, and now that I am home, my mother feels at a loss on a Sunday afternoon with no-one to write to.

As the years went by and good friends became better friends, I began sending weekly faxes to them too. Somehow it felt as if we had never been apart.

When email came along the numbers of people I correspond with mushroomed out of all proportion. The notes I send are shorter and full of typos but the thought is there and old friends are never far from my thoughts.

Keeping in touch makes your support team, even if its members are distant, feel close at hand. When we first moved to Stavanger it was as if I took my friend Gill with me. We communicated so regularly at first that I didn't feel quite so alone in a strange place. When she went to the United Arab Emirates I was there for her, ensuring I replied to her emails straight away, giving support and soothing comments.

Keeping in touch is much more than a card at Christmas.

• Tip No 5 – Retain Your Identity

At a recent workshop on 'enriching your life', we were all asked to draw a picture of how we perceived ourselves. It was amazing how many people drew themselves with their children and families. I drew myself holding a briefcase in one hand and two children in the other.

How do you picture yourself? Many people are fulfilled being a homemaker and mother alone. Others are satisfied with a demanding career and little social life. Draw a picture of how you see yourself now and then another of how you would like to be. Have you exchanged the baby for the briefcase or a tennis racket?

It is important for you to be able to be yourself despite living in a foreign location and an international community. Try to pinpoint what elements you need to have in your life in order to function as a complete and contented person, and then make every effort to ensure that you make time for them too. Be kind to yourself and you will, in turn, be kinder to everyone around you.

• Tip No 6 – Treat Yourself

I heard a story the other day about a family who went to work and live overseas with the sole objective of saving every penny they earned. They lived like paupers with hardly any furniture and without a television or stereo, had no social life and never went on holiday. They went home rich. Or did they? New experiences enrich your life in a different way from money. It seems a waste to have the opportunity of experiencing another culture at first hand and then not to take it.

Many expatriates, though not all, do have financial incentives for living abroad. Many receive generous travel allowances. If you are homesick it is easy to grab every airline ticket and head for home, but if you do that you are missing the chance to explore the world at someone else's expense. Why not take a longer 'home' leave in the summer and a shorter trip during the winter to somewhere closer.

Living away from your roots is not easy. You need to feel that your sacrifices are worthwhile and that there are true advantages to a nomadic lifestyle.

Treat yourself to the opera if you live in Vienna, or spend a night at the Oriental Hotel if you live in Bangkok. Buy yourself some rosewood furniture from Hong Kong or a dirt cheap Discovery in Dubai. These little treats soften the blow, and while they lower your bank balance they do lift your spirits.

• Tip No 7 – Do Something Different

Every new posting brings with it a host of opportunities. If you find your-self in Indonesia with a fleet of servants, then you have time to take that distance learning course you have been talking about. If you find your-self in a land of sand dunes why not take up sandskiing or learn to dune bash in a four-wheel-drive? If you have taken on a live-in babysitter there is no reason why you shouldn't join the local choral society or drama group. Rehearsals thrice weekly are no longer a problem.

Take advantages of the things you are able to do in the new location that you would never do at home. In Dubai and Muscat my husband played rhythm and lead guitar with a series of rock bands. His group, Mother Superior and the Bad Habits seized the opportunity to back up The Manfreds when they came on tour, and earned good money enter-taining everyone at the company Christmas dinner too. Back in England, he is lucky to join in a jam session at the local pub. Being a big fish in a small pond gave me the chance to write features for a local woman's magazine despite my lack of experience. In the end I had to use two pseudonyms I was so busy. Back in England the chances of my finding a slot in a woman's monthly magazine is slim, if not impossible.

Being creative is a marvellous outlet for your emotions. Expatriate communities are often packed with talented, bored women, who would rather teach sculpture or silk painting for free than sit at home unable to obtain a work permit. Take advantage of these cut price courses. Sometimes you will only have to pay for your own materials.

Living in a new and exciting culture can do wonders for your imagi-nation. It broadens the mind and fills your vocabulary, sound and sight banks with new items that you can pull out when you are creating music, words or pictures. Try keeping a diary as well as a photograph album and videos, so that you can store your rich variety experiences for the future. You never know – they could earn you some money one day.

• Tip No 8 – Call it Home

Remember Alice? I told you about her in the section on proactivity. Well, Alice, and her family have been on the move almost constantly. During this time they have lived in several locations in England, Scotland, America and Norway. And, subsequent to a few month's settling-in peri-od, in each new place, Alice has always worked out of the home. But one thing stands out above all others that has ensured that their life is as settled as possible – wherever they are living is They could have put down roots in almost any country or city they have inhabited, and insist that *home* is *now*. They take their furniture and all their possessions on every move, and it was not until the move from a large Norwegian house to Surrey was imminent that they finally said goodbye to the pool table.

Hankering after a place where you used to belong does no-one any good, least of all you. So make the place you live in now your home and personalise it as best you can with memorabilia from past lives, trips and people. Blend the Indian furniture with the Bedouin rugs and Turkish copper and make each place you live uniquely your own. Make huge collages of the faces and places from each assignment and take pleasure in reliving those magic moments whenever you glance at it. For if home is where the hearth is then the heart should follow too.

• Tip No 9 – Explore

I can remember vividly the hours it would take to pack our four wheel drive for weekend camping trips into the desert when we lived in Oman. After I had packed drinks coolboxes and food coolboxes, found lilos and pumps, buckets spades, cooking utensils, tents and sunshades into the boot, Ian would roll up from work, ready to jump into his shorts and leap behind the wheel. Then, arriving home in the dark on a Friday evening (for Fridays are Sundays in that part of the world), hot, tired, thirsty and encrusted with sand and sea water, we would laboriously unpack, desand and rinse everything all over again. I used to swear it took more time to pack and unpack, drive there and back and finally pitch and unpitch camp than we actually spent there relaxing. But it was always worth it. To lie back in the warm air, listening to the waves, staring up at a velvet starscape watching out for shooting stars was a rare privilege. To have stayed at home with Sky TV and a take-away could not compare.

It can be so much easier to stay at home, but never so exciting nor enriching an experience. Diaries and photograph albums, memories even, are not made in your sitting room or front garden. Get out and about, feed your soul and develop your conversation. Learn about local sights or nature and really experience a country from the inside.

Day trips can last you a lifetime.

• Tip No 10 – Get Involved

Saying 'yes' is a much repeated message in this book. And getting involved is about saying 'yes'. It is about giving up your free time to volunteer for committees you care about. It is about meeting regularly with people of like mind and doing something that interests you. It could be the school parent teacher association, or the arts centre. If you are not a committee kind of person then you can still say yes to being in a squash ladder or to joining in to play pétanque in France. If you don't like committees and hate sports then you could join in a sewing bee or take cookery classes. Getting involved in something means that you meet people. People become friends. Friends become your support team and your social life. When you are involved you start to belong. Belonging is the objective of us all.

Here I go advocating that you all have to join something, when I know only too well how much I hate making that first step. Even at a newcomers coffee morning of the Petroleum Wives Club I found myself tongue-tied and terrified of having to introduce myself. But the moment I had opened my mouth and said the first word the ice was broken and in a flash someone had handed me the telephone number of a potential babysitter in my area. I was off. I duly joined the PWC, attended one more coffee morning three weeks later and never went there again. Because three weeks later one contact had led to another and I was far too busy.

So take that first step towards involvement in just one thing, and even if that group is not your ideal choice, it can be the catalyst you need and the start of belonging.

Joanna would like to share the following with you :

Federation of American Women's Clubs Overseas
http://www.fawco.co.org/clubtabl.htm

Resident Abroad Subscriptions
PO Box 387 Haywards Heath
RH16 3GS
UK

British Council Information Centre
Tel : 0044-(0)161 957 7755

Arrivals Quotations

My feelings go up and down like a seesaw. One moment I am feeling on top of the world: arriving in Dubai to be given VIP treatment, speeding through the city gazing at the incredible white buildings. Then the next moment I am down again: feeling so tired, not coping with the jet lag nor the obligatory late nights attending 'welcome' functions while coping with three tired, excited and demanding children.

Gill Beckwith in the United Arab Emirates.

We watched agape as the cages of live chickens from Azerbazhan, the wicker baskets of melons from Armenia did the tour of the luggage carousel. Waiting for our own Samsonite cases we watched African students leap to retrieve their sacking and string-bound chattels.

Bobby Meyer in the Former Soviet Union.

It is six months now since we arrived but instead of all the things I had hoped to do, I am still busy 'moving'. We seem to take one step forward and two steps back. Oliver, never the easiest child to feed, has had to give up the Bran Flakes, which were previously the mainstay of his diet. Fortunately he has been weaned onto Oat Crunchies.

Nicki Chambury arriving in Miri, Sarawak.

When I first arrived in Houston I felt like I was living in a movie. Everything about the place had been portrayed in films before. Wide streets, big hoardings, drive-in cinemas. The feeling didn't wear off for two years.

Alice Hurley in the United States of America.

Arriving is a bit like running off a cliff, cartoon-style. You keep on running at speed on thin air and are fine until you look down and lose your faith. Then you fall fast and far.

Christine Yates in Germany.

I just put my head down and get into a routine as quickly as possible, accepting all invitations. I also moan at my husband a lot.

Hilary Milne in Norway after 16 years of Cairo, Russia and more.

We had a growing sense of euphoria at having arrived after all that anticipation, then a growing sensation that Madagascar is somewhat different from Hertfordshire.

Mark Eadie in Madagascar.

But Not This
by Christine Yates, English in Germany

Why is it that at thirty-four
I want to scream and run amok
And be perverse and slam the door
And do those things that I ought not?
I want no duty, must or should

No really ought or said I would –
Instead I'd rather scream and swear
And shock with words I never use
Or hurl down insults and abuse
On those whose faces I must bear.

But at my age it feels not right –
To employ adolescent tools,
To rail against the wooden rules,
The moribund smiles and easy truths,
And yet?
Which other rules am I to use?

'What DO you want?' he asks with a kiss.
'I JUST DON'T KNOW,' I say.
'But not this.'

The Moving Conspiracy
by Sandra Haube McDonnell, American in Norway
Leaving for your first posting can be hell.

I am an organized person. I like to know where things are. I like things to be put in order. Normally, I am not a control freak or a raving lunatic. Really, I'm not. I only became a maniac after I discovered the evil conspiracy against me. You think I'm kidding? You explain it.

My husband is in the Army. I expected to have to move. I was ready for it. Despite the assurances that we would be staying put, I knew better. I was ready. So, when they told us we were moving to Norway, it came as a small shock, but I didn't come unglued. That didn't happen until the weather, the movers, the carpet guy and the government got involved. Blame them, not me.

As the move drew nearer, we were beginning to panic a little. We had no official orders, which meant that anything could change at any moment. Being the good military wife that I am, I bought sweaters and wool socks, catalogued our belongings and started organizing the house. I tried not to let the uncertainty bother me. I even applied for my passport. And then the government closed. Yes, it actually closed for an indeterminate length of time because the politicians in Washington were acting like spoiled children. I still didn't let it bother me. When they re-opened, I called and made it clear that I had a deadline. They said they'd try. Then the government closed again. It didn't look good.

Meanwhile, the Army decided to send only my husband. They thought that as newlyweds, we'd like a two year break from one another. This sent my husband over the edge. I'm not kidding. He wasn't upset, or stressed out, he was ballistic. Needless to say, I wasn't much calmer. Still, by yelling at the right people, we got it taken care of. And then my passport arrived, having been processed during the three working days between government shut-downs. Things were looking better.

Next came phase two of the plot against us. Snow. You heard me, snow. Maryland never gets more than six inches of snow per winter. It usually comes in one to two inch doses and isn't hard to deal with. Instead, this particular winter we had storm after storm with snow accumulations over a foot at a time. Everything was closed for weeks on end. Still, I didn't let it bother me. We'd had enough trouble, I knew the storms would just send snow on either side of our packing and moving dates. I was sure of it. The week we were supposed to leave for Norway arrived. It was ushered in by more than a foot of snow. The movers didn't show up. I didn't panic. I called about six hundred times and finally got someone. I sweetly asked when they would be coming. They promised to arrive the next day. And then the next. By Wednesday, the owner knew my name and voice and addressed me as 'sigh . . . Now Mrs. McDonnell . . . ' He promised they'd be there tomorrow.

'That's what you said yesterday!' Okay, maybe I was a little short with him. But our plane was leaving on Friday.

Wednesday was also the day we'd arranged to have carpet laid in the basement. From the time we'd been notified of the possible move to Norway, my husband and a friend had been feverishly doing construction on the basement to make it into a usable room. The extra space was an attractive feature for potential tenants. In fact, our tenants had one year-old twins and would not have rented the house without the extra room. The carpet store didn't even open until noon, then said they really didn't know what the schedule would be.

'I don't care. I am leaving the country. The carpet must be laid tomorrow!' I think I stunned the poor man. He gulped for air, made a few strangled sounds and then said they'd be there the next day.

The movers and carpeting taken care of I tried to relax. We even went out for a farewell dinner with friends. I took a few deep breaths and readied myself to deal with the struggle of packing and carpeting and turning the house over to tenants all on the same day. It would be tough, but I knew we could do it. The one problem left was finding a home for our dog, who was too old to make it through the Norwegian quarantine system. Everyone loved our dog, but no one wanted to be his new owner. Believe me, I asked, begged everyone I knew repeatedly. Still, I couldn't worry about that at the moment. It would work out. It had to.

The movers, fearing another call from the deranged Mrs McDonnell, showed up promptly and began packing quickly and carefully. I was unprepared to have four large men frightened by me, but willing to accept such a thing if it meant they packed my belongings more carefully. Then, the final straw – the carpet man called to cancel.

'Sorry lady, can't make it.' He sounded so unconcerned.

'I don't care. You have to lay the carpet today. I AM LEAVING THE COUNTRY TOMORROW.'

'You can always let your tenants handle it. We can try to come next week.'

Okay, I came a little unglued. Suddenly, having that carpet laid was the most important thing in my life. My poor brain was too overwhelmed to accept defeat. I could not deal with trying to create plan B at that late date.

'The tenants are paying to move into a house with a carpeted basement. I paid you to deal with this already. There is no alternative. YOU HAVE TO COME AND INSTALL THE CARPETING TODAY.' I didn't think I was shouting. And then I noticed the movers. They were all standing still, staring at me.

'Wow,' one of them said quietly. Upon seeing me staring back, they all got back to work, quickly. Screaming like a maniac appeared to have inspirational affects on the movers. Not only that, it caused a miracle that made it possible for the carpet man to get there after all. Being a shrew can have its upside.

That taken care of, there was still the matter of our homeless pet. He really was a terrific dog and he deserved a loving home. A friend, one I'd recently met at church, came by to see if he could help.

Without an ounce of shame, I pressed my loving pet on him.

'Your daughters will love him. He's house trained and loving and makes a wonderful pet. He'd love to have two little girls to spoil him. PLEASE!! HE HAS NO HOME!' Our new friend, being an ex-military member and a decent guy, saw all the signs of stress overload and agreed. The dog had a new home, with 24 hours to spare.

The movers and carpet people left in time to allow us half an hour to clean up for the tenants. I have never cleaned so fast in my life. I put my sister to work too, knowing we could only get through it together. And so we were transformed into cleaning machines. We grunted to each other in passing or when one of us needed the other's cleaning fluid. Beyond that, talk was brushed aside and cleaning occupied our every thought. We threw away the last bag of trash as the tenants were parking their car.

I sighed with relief, knowing we had beaten the conspiracy – or at least that's what I thought. Mother nature tried one last assault, dumping six more inches of snow overnight. They closed the airport all morning. Our flight, which left at six pm, was still a possibility. When it re-opened we took a death defying drive, courtesy of a friend, to the airport. The major highways were still under several inches of snow, and the other drivers seemed not to notice. I closed my eyes and held on.

When our plane finally took off, with us aboard, I breathed deeply for the first time in a week. We did it. Nothing on the other side could be as harrowing as getting out had been. At first it seemed like we'd left the conspiracy behind. We found a nice house reasonably quickly, and began to settle in. Then, when we'd been in Norway just three months, the Army informed us that we would be deployed to Croatia for six months, leaving me alone in a strange country. I guess it took the perpetrators of the conspiracy a few months to find us, but they seem to be back at it.

Arrival Survival
by Sarah Leighton, English in Guam
The joy of flying with three children – and a tactless husband.

Terminal three, Heathrow. Check-in. The perfectly coiffed girl on the check-in desk tells us that there has been a mix-up over seat allocation. One of us will have to sit ten rows back. Of course each of our three children vociferously refuse to sit next to strangers. In less than a second my husband selflessly volunteers for the lone seat. His rare selflessness is tempered with a sly look of triumph.

Luggage 30kg overweight, which leaves us £10 short. Husband swears - not under his breath. Grandparents embarrassed into making hurried whip-round. They pay the excess while shooting calculating glances at the shopping bags bulging out of our newly purchased duffle.

Tearful farewells. Last hug till next year. Through Passport Control. The children demand to visit the restaurant. They fight over the last remaining doughnut. The people on the neighbouring table hope they're on different flight. We sigh. It is only 21 hours before we get 'home'. Husband slips away for crafty fag.

On board. The children each scramble to get the sole window seat. The first punch is thrown. Then the second. Middle-child wins. Husband slopes off to his single seat whereupon he promises unconvincingly to swap half-way. The in-flight entertainment is not yet operating so the children demand snacks and comics. The air stewardess offers me a newspaper. I chance it. My youngest child takes one look at my paper and immediately whines to have a book read to him.

Announcement by captain. Minor mechanical fault. Slight delay. Brittle smiles from the hostesses who then stride to the back of the plane. We spend two hours on the tarmac. The children finish their snacks and comics and start sniggering at rude jokes. Then they start sniggering at rude jokes about other passengers.

Fault fixed. Plane takes off and the atmosphere visibly calms. Husband comes up for the first time since boarding and pats the children's heads indulgently. Then he returns to his seat. The in-flight entertainment comes on and the children play computer games. My youngest can't do it and whines for help. I can't do it. I whine to the eldest for help. I swap places with eldest. I swap handbag and newspaper for crumpled comic and assorted sticky wrappers. Five minutes later I swap back again.

Dinner arrives. Youngest immediately bursting to go to loo. He can't wait five minutes. He can't wait five seconds and slips under his tray towards the floor. As he crawls through my legs he knocks over my red wine. My new cream shirt proves very absorbent. I try attracting a hostess. I finish my first course then start on the second. I am now desperate for that wine refill. Youngest climbs over other passengers to get past the hostess and trolley. Crawls through my legs just as I am receiving that wine refill. Amazingly it stays secure. Instead he knocks his own Coca-Cola onto his seat. Then he refuses to sit on it.

Hostess too busy to clear trays. Youngest stands on seat and glares balefully at the passenger behind. The passenger attempts an embarrassed smile. Youngest's glare is now hostile. The hostess clears our trays. I notice that the red wine stain has dried. The Coca Cola hasn't so I use a blanket to cover the seat.

Then to my horror I realise that the children are enthralled by an explicit sex scene on the video. I forbid them to watch. Youngest dozes off. I doze off. I wake up to find the children enthralled by a different explicit sex scene on the video. I confiscate their headsets.

Desperate for another drink. Children are bickering and whinging again. It is definitely time to swap places with my husband. He is in such a deep coma that he fails to respond to a vicious pinch. I return resentfully to my seat and sleep fitfully. I am woken by coarse laughter from the two older children. I threaten them discreetly. Next time I am woken by a fight. I hit the two children discreetly. Unfortunately my attempts at discretion are rapidly undermined by their loud accusations of child abuse.

Begin descent. Husband in panic. He has forgotten to fill in our great wad of immigration forms. He yells across ten rows of passengers because he can't remember the children's middle names. Then he can't remember their dates of birth. Oh no, he can't remember mine either. Now all the passengers know my age.

Off plane. We wait in the Aliens queue. Under my breath I menacingly tell my eldest child not to express adverse opinions about the Immigration Officer.

Through Immigration. We wait for our luggage. There appear to be no trolleys. Apparently they are all at Departures.

Frantic search for my duty-free bag. Find the gin. Who needs ice?

Sick in Stavanger
by Linda March, English in Norway
A kidney stone is the last thing you need, especially when you
have just arrived.

One of my major concerns on relocating with young children to a new country was, of course, the quality of medical care – would it be up to scratch should the need arise? One of my dearest hopes was that we would never have to find out. On moving to Stavanger, Norway, I discovered that, as so often in my life, my concerns were as ill-founded as my hopes were confounded.

Nine days after arrival I could find my way unaided, or with the help of the local Kartbok, to the British School and to a supermarket. I also said 'hello' to three people. In my husband's judgement I was fully settled and could handle the house and children while he went offshore for two weeks. Never mind the fact that he would be away longer than my feet had been on Norwegian soil.

As I waved goodbye at the heliport I felt a twist in my stomach. Strange, I thought, we decided long before to halt the production of more offspring. Seventeen hours of hard labour, an attempt at ventouse delivery without pain relief and a Caesarean section had heralded the birth of our first child five years before. Could relocation to Norway, with its scenic fjords and majestic mountains, have been the catalyst required for a spot of recklessness? I belched. Possibly not.

Driving off manfully on the wrong side of the road and clutching the wheel with every spasm of pain, I cursed those strange dumplings I'd been talked into eating and remembered that the best way to cure a tummy bug is to starve it out. My resolve held for 36 hours until I was no longer sure which was causing the greater pain – hunger or upset stomach – and recklessly ate a dry water biscuit. Almost immediately I was struck to my knees on the kitchen floor while attempting to decipher Norwegian cooking instructions for unfamiliar fish cakes for the children's supper. Not surprisingly a migraine jumped on the bandwagon and I limped off to bed.

After two sleepless nights writhing on the relative comfort of the heated bathroom floor, I – stalwart as I am – offshore widow, experienced at coping with disasters alone, realised that even I had never been this alone before. I was forced, for the first time in my life to give in and request that my husband do the unthinkable – put his family before the company and come home.

Much to my relief he was on the next helicopter and home within three and a half hours. Much to his relief, since he seemed under the misapprehension that he had been summoned from duty by a wimpish migraine, which would not go down at all well with the company. And 36 hours later I was admitted to the emergency room at Stavanger General Hospital.

As my only previous hospitalisation had occurred in a British Maternity Hospital I was certainly not prepared for two of the Norwegian admissions procedures. Firstly, I was presented with a perfectly decent, perfectly comfortable hospital gown – no back opening leaving an embarrassing two inch gap from neck to rear, not so starched that every movement resulted in painful chafing. It was even a pretty colour and decorated with flowers. I stared at it in disbelief before being met with my second shock. I was requested to take my temperature by a nurse who was aghast when I started to place the thermometer in my mouth. She struggled to find the correct English quickly enough – 'Bottom!' she finally said triumphantly, 'You put it in your bottom.' My husband and children brightened visibly. This would liven things up. I stared at the door. I wanted to go home. No, not just up the road to the rented house in Røyneberg, but real home. Suddenly a chafing hospital gown seemed a small price to pay for the luxury of a British thermometer tucked comfortably under my tongue. But the deed had to be done.

Once the formalities were complete and it seemed unlikely that further entertaining diversions would be on offer, my yawning husband and children went home, leaving me to await removal to the ward. The strangeness of being alone in a foreign hospital, still unsure what was wrong with me and what might be done to me, was alleviated by a comfortingly familiar touch. I was left lying in an ante room for two hours before a nurse looked in and said in surprise, 'Are you still here? I think they've forgotten about you.' I smiled nostalgically. Apart from the accent it could have been home.

The next two days passed in a whirl of new experiences. I was required to pass urine into a receptacle suitably sized and shaped for ladies. A nurse unpacked my belongings for me into my locker, and expressed surprise at my nightdress, towel and toiletries. I discovered why when I was presented with a clean nightdress, towels and a sort of boxer shorts, (sympathetically marked 'small'). In addition, there were soap and shampoo in the bathrooms, pillows on the bed and clean cutlery at every meal. Previously, if more than one pillow was required then it had to be brought from home. I would also have been issued with a set of cutlery on admission for which I was responsible until my discharge. I took the abundant personal supplies in Norway to mean that inhabitants of one of the wealthiest countries in the world don't need to steal.

And as for the nurses, they were in abundant supply too. Quite often, in our pleasant four-bedded ward, there were more nurses than patients. They brought drinks, picked up magazines, plumped the pillows, chatted and reprimanded me for not buzzing when I needed them. Instead of waking us at six for a brief prodding before leaving us blinking in the bright lights of another long, tedious hospital day, they woke us leisurely around eight.

However, all good things come to an end. My condition improved and it was decided that I had passed a kidney stone. I had been the only person in the hospital without blonde hair and had unwittingly killed half the patients on life support machines because I had been unable to understand the warnings about not using mobile phones, but it had been a wonderful two days and quite wasted on a poorly person. I resolved that next time things got rough I would stage a neat collapse outside the doors.

Hospitalisation in a foreign country can be a traumatic experience. My husband had been faced with the fact that his children go to school and require clean, ironed clothes and a packed lunch to do so. Sometimes it's harder on the relatives.

A Testing Time
by Gillian Taylor, English in Egypt
More than just a test of driving skills.

My initial reaction was that someone had made a mistake. How could a British Driving Licence not be accepted as conclusive proof of my expert driving skills? What did they mean I'd have to do another test in Cairo to earn the Egyptian equivalent?

Well, I very soon learnt that driving in Cairo is a hugely different game to motoring in comparatively sedate London. Arriving under cover of night I had been truly fooled into supposing that the traffic was light and the roads ridiculously wide. When Simon, my husband of less than 48 hours, happily kissed me goodbye the next morning I was blissfully unaware that day break had already brought chaos to the streets. Weeks before our test date we were assured by Simon's company that they would rent a small car for us to drive during the test. They didn't advise doing it in the big four wheel drive that we had just purchased. That, in itself, sounded foreboding.

On the fateful morning that Simon went to collect the keys for our hire car he was met by a vacant expression. 'Maalish!' they told him. This means never mind. The car would still be at the test station at 1o'clock. So we set off in the 20 year old Peugeot 505 estate car that belonged to our company escort Hamdi.

To my surprise the test centre was located under a bridge. I assumed that we would be taken out on to the roads but was completely wrong. We were kept waiting two hours to do the theory part of the test. While we chatted, several

Filipino immigrants sat swotting up and testing each other on the international road signs. Hamdi signalled to us to enter the inspector's room. Inside the inspector was enjoying a Turkish coffee and The Egyptian Gazette. When he was ready he pointed at random to a few signs on his wall and grinned, looking sure that he had caught us out. At every reply he smiled and then quickly pointed to another sign. He thought he was trying to confuse us – but it was obvious that he didn't speak a word of English so we could have said anything.

We were instructed to wait outside, back under the bridge, for the practical test. It didn't look as if our car had arrived. Hamdi's expression was not very reassuring. 'Inshallah' he said, 'God willing, it will be here.'

At 12.40 pm, 20 minutes ahead of schedule, I was instructed to get into my car. Protestations that I didn't have one were ignored and I found myself in the driver's seat of Hamdi's antique.

Four pairs of traffic cones had been placed in a zigzag shape under the bridge and I was told to drive first forwards and then backwards through them. A crowd had assembled from nowhere. Going forwards was manageable but when I didn't move back for a few minutes, Hamdi came over to help me yank the unwilling the gear stick into reverse. I checked the wing mirrors – but found that there weren't any, so I turned to look out of the back window. All I could see was the back of my seat. The cushions had no springs and I had sunk about six inches when I first sat down. I tried to picture where the cones were and turned the wheel. There was a loud crunch - I had flattened the first cone! The inspector gesticulated wildly at me and then at Hamdi.

'Go and wait over there,' he yelled in Arabic indicating that I should get out of the car immediately.

Simon, being six feet and two inches tall, was able to see over the back of the seat, but he also just touched a cone. Hamdi told us, with a very kind and totally unsurprised look on his face, not to worry. He said he knew this inspector and often 'dealt with him'.

After witnessing several more similar fiascoes we drove off to a rendezvous with the inspector. Hamdi left us in the car and walked off with a handful of our Egyptian Pounds. He returned minutes later, beaming.

'Congratulations, you passed, and I managed to get you a 20% discount! too!'

Hairdressers Make Your Toes Curl

by Linda March, English in Norway

Now you have reason to be terrified of strange hairstylists.

Three months into our first experience of expatism in an excruciatingly expensive Scandinavian country, I was beginning to learn the ropes. I had driven up snowy mountains, learned how to 'coffee morning' and how to feel uneasy on entering a supermarket with less than £100 in my purse. In other words I had everything sussed – well almost everything. I had yet to find the courage to visit a hairdresser.

My reluctance to take the plunge was born out of two things. Firstly, my attachment to my hairdresser back home: Helen and I had been together for over eight years. She'd seen me through a tricky moment with a floral hair piece on my wedding day. She'd given me the pregnancy-manual-recommended trim two weeks before the due date of my first child so I'd still look good when pushing and panting and entertaining visitors (well, okay, even Helen couldn't do the impossible). She'd sympathised with my post-natal hair loss and found enterprising ways to make less look more, and, most importantly, during the last four years, she'd been supporting me through the trauma of greyness with a large bottle of vegetable dye. Nobody could take her place. Nobody. Secondly, I'd been warned about the local hairdressers by several people. Not only did they charge frightening amounts of money to trim a child's fringe, but they did not take kindly to being told what to do. In addition, I'd heard that they tended to specialise in one style and that you came out with that style, regardless of your preference. The only solution seemed to be to hang around outside all the hairdressers in town until I found one with people emerging in a style I favoured.

By Christmas things were desperate and we were all very shaggy indeed. However, it seemed that help was at hand in the form of Damir, John's Bosnian friend. Damir had a friend called Vanessa who had been a hairdresser back in Mostar. Her qualifications weren't recognised in Norway so she worked from home on the black economy, styling the hair of all the local refugees.

I asked John about Damir's wife's hair and he said it was 'fine'. Of course, this was a foolish question as his judgement on women's hairstyles is not something I had ever considered valuing before. In fact, when pressed, he could describe neither style nor colour, but maintained it was definitely 'fine'.

Anxious, but with vision rapidly declining, I agreed to take the plunge and we all trooped off to Vanessa's. We stopped on the way to collect Damir, so that he could show us the way, introduce us, and perform a more important role as we were later to discover.

Vanessa's little flat was rather sad. It was our first glimpse of anything less than wealth here. All her possessions were on two shelves against the wall in a bare sitting room. But the atmosphere was cheerful enough as several Bosnians were drinking strong coffee and chatting noisily.

The 'salon' was a tiny room bearing a white plastic garden chair and a mirror placed just too high on the wall to be of any use to the clients. As usual, my older daughter had to be first and she plonked herself in the chair. It was now that we discovered Damir's role – no, not sweeping up the hair trimmings – interpreting!

Being rather a reserved person and used to the unwritten law of confidentiality between a woman and her coiffeuse, I had never discussed my hairdressing requirements in the presence of my husband, far less several interested Bosnian strangers. I began to panic as I wondered whether Damir's excellent engineering English was up to his ladies' hairdressing English. My terse 'just a trim' took about five minutes to translate and was accompanied by all manner of Bosnian handwaving. I had failed to notice that he and Vanessa's husband had the shortest hair ever seen on a non-bald person and I hoped that three years in this new land hadn't rubbed off on Vanessa and made her start practising only that one style.

I need not have worried. She made a good job of the children's hair and I drank very strong, very sweet coffee while wondering how I looked and waiting for John to emerge. Like many ex-servicemen of his generation, he has spent the last ten years making up for having been condemned to a short back and sides at a time when the rest of the youth of the western world had boasted long locks flowing halfway down their backs. Since then, although his leg is often pulled about it, his longish curly hair has been his trade mark. Or should I say 'had been'.

It seems strange that Damir's excellent command of English did not extend to 'not too short' or maybe my fears of the one style were well founded. The wicked grin that Damir exchanged with his friends may hold the answer.

When my shorn and downcast husband emerged our children fell off their chairs laughing at his ears, of which they had been in blissful ignorance until that moment. Whilst I reflected on the sad loss of childhood innocence, Damir informed us of the amazingly low cost of this adventure.

As John will now only need his hair cutting once a year, we should be quids in.

Forced To Fly

Inflight Quotations

The nearest city was 50 miles away and a two hour drive from our isolated compound where 25 families lived. We were not all expatriates and we all socialized together. We had no community services, just a coconut grove, with palms on one side and the ocean on the other.

Colleen Macdonald in Trinidad.

Even when I was settled, it never felt 'ordinary'. There was always something bizarre or unusual going on – like finding an alligator in the back garden or going to a rodeo.

Alice Hurley in the United States of America.

I had learned the rules of expatriate society and how to fit in so that relationships with people were improved.

Susan Valentine in The Sultanate of Oman.

I could remember my local cashpoint number but not the one back 'home'. I no longer needed to take the street plan with me and knew the whereabouts of all the public lavatories.

Sarah Buxton in Paris.

I spent 13 years there but never felt really settled. They say that you are not truly accepted until a Swiss family invites you for a cheese fondue. With a cheese fondue you all dip your wooden sticks with speared bread cube into a communcal pot. Then you put the cheese-covered bread in your mouth. Then you spear a new piece of bread and begin again. This is very unhygenic and very un-Swiss. Ergo only family and very close friends are allowed to be fellow-dippers. Needless to say I was never invited.

Paul Cleary in Switzerland.

Being settled is the feeling that you know where you are, who you are and where you are going, what you want and where to get it. It happens one morning when you wake up and realise you have overcome culture shock and can throw yourself wholeheartedly at the day.

Christine Yates in Germany..

I had come to accept the bureaucracy and the endless paperwork.

Mark Eadie in The Netherlands.

Our research has shown that it takes six years to truly settle in.

Anne Copeland, Intercultural Exchange Institute, USA.

Dancing
by Elizabeth Lavers, English in Africa

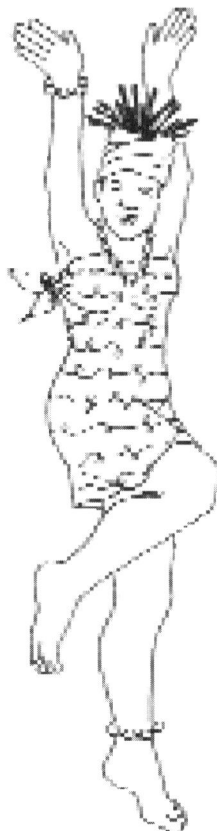

You should hear us laugh, you should hear us sing
And – and oh – but oh, you should see us dance!
We dance in the womb to the beat of the heart
And are brought forth dancing with cries of surprise
To dance on our sister's sinuous backs
On the way to the stream or the market place;
We dance to the tap of a hammer, a spoon
To the slapping of paddles, to a drip from the thatch
To the rattle and clang of a train on the rails
To the sound of the pounding of black shea butter
Where women are laughing and working together;
We dance for a wedding, for the pleasure of life
For a chief at a feast, for an old friend dead
For a traveller returned, for a child newborn
For no good reason or in God's good praise.
As our eyes grow dim, in sorrow and pain
Though our bodies grow old, we go dancing on
With our children's children, their neighbours and wives
Without even stopping for our burial day
To the pulsing beat of the tireless drums –
Till at length our steps make no pattern of sound
Not a rustle, not a whisper in the listening wind
And we fade like shadows on our noiseless feet
And all that is left
            is a memory
                  dancing.

Visitors from Hell

by Susan Ventris, English in Norway
Why do your parents always bring so much baggage?

Picture this . . . The perfect visitors from back home arrive at your expatriate door. They're laden with bulging suitcases crammed with jars of Marmite, freezer food from Marks and Spencer and catering packs of Crunchie bars. They stagger beneath the weight of boxes containing a Fisher Price kitchen and a full size trampoline. In their hand luggage they've gamely smuggled six litres of spirits, then declare a thirst for tap water.

You love these visitors. They have their own hire car, and use it. They depart early each morning on sightseeing trips, returning at nightfall just in time to help the children with their homework. Their favourite meal is beans on toast, which they cook themselves. They're fluent in the local language and translate your awkward documents for you. They stay no longer than 48 hours.

These visitors are not your relatives

Your relatives arrive with suitcases crammed with medications and a vast wardrobe for themselves, catering for all eventualities from Arctic snowstorms to blistering heat. They forget the duty free, then head straight for your gin bottle. You feel a brief flurry of excitement at the sight of a Sainsbury's pie, but it's turkey and ham and you've been vegetarian for years.

Once on foreign soil, your parents lose all power of independent movement. One of these days they'll start following you into the bathroom. They never hire a car, or if they do, they're too nervous to drive it. They lie in bed until 10 o'clock while you sort out the kids and do the school run. Then they arise, raring to go. Each day they expect you to take them on excursions which leave you perpetually exhausted. Once home after these jaunts, their energy deserts them, and they flop into an armchair while you cook the evening meal.

They bring their medical histories with them. When healthy, they complain vaguely of the change in the air, but they're seldom healthy. They come armed to the teeth with medicines from Boots, but still manage to fall ill with monotonous regularity. If that bad back, frozen shoulder or gippy tummy is going to play up, it's ten to a penny it'll do so under your roof. Usually all three strike at once, and you struggle to suppress the natural resentment you feel when faced with an ancient Quasimodo with a severe stomach bug.

And they're forgetful. They forget about time zones and ring you in the middle of the night to tell you when they'll be arriving. They forget which side of the road to drive on, or they forget their driving licence, and can't drive at all. They promise to bring a recording of the latest episode of your favourite TV serial, but they forget how to work the video, so you get a documentary about the mating habits of wildebeest.

They have inflexible attitudes to food. Your diet of choice may now be vegan, or heavily influenced by the time you spent in the Far East, but for a fortnight you're back to a solid diet of meat and two vegetables. They look wounded if you don't produce a pudding.

Eating out is no alternative. They eat ruinously expensive meals in restaurants because they can't convert back. Educated in pre-decimal days, they know precisely how many chains there are to a furlong, or peck to a bushel, but are vague about the purpose of a decimal point. One friend's father ordered a bottle of wine costing £150 while his son was in the lavatory.

Their ways are not your ways. Brought up in post-war austerity, they tiptoe around closing doors and switching off lights, then break their ankles in the darkened stairwell. They bath the kids in an inch of tepid water. They're too economical to hire a car, but surprisingly liberal with the sherry bottle.

And then there's the bad behaviour. Not theirs – although that's bad enough – but your own. One summer, driven to desperate measures, I sent my parents on an eight hour trip down a Norwegian fjord, armed only with a packet of polo mints. They were glad of these later, when they discovered that there was no food on board.

Parents are the worst species of visitors. You know they'll be coming back. The trouble is, we love them. So for a fortnight a year, we put up with their foibles, discovering a few of our own in the process. Our guilt binds us to them. In our hearts, we know that no crimes they could commit while under our roof for a fortnight could compare to those we perpetrated while under theirs.

For 18 years or so, we ground rusks into their carpets, crayoned on their wallpaper, and roller-skated down their hall. Later, we played loud rock music at all hours and grappled with leather-jacketed youths on their doorstep, while they lay awake, fretting. The horrible behaviour of our own children is a chilling reminder of our own past sins.

Our parents, because they never change, remind us that we have. We remember that we weren't always this well-travelled, this well-paid, this worldly. They're a yardstick of our success, a measure of how far we've come.

This is why we try to sound pleased when they ring to arrange their next visit; a phone call which always comes at three o'clock in the morning.

Expat Pets

by Louise Rankin, English in Norway

Pets get a raw deal when their owners move on.

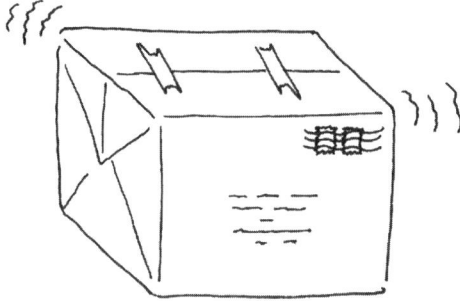

You've only got one Louise, haven't you?' says a shrill voice from across the coffee table. I look down, rapidly crossing my arms in the vague fear that a mastectomy has taken place without my knowledge.

'One what?' I enquire, having established nature's balanced fullness remains.

'Cat, of course,' spikes the voice.

'Mmmn,' I mutter, heaving a sigh of relief.

'Well you could always take another one. You see Missy's just had five kittens and we don't know what to do with them,' squeaks the voice in desperation.

How many times have you been asked this same question and been tempted to rescue the plight of a good friend in a recognisable situation? Invariably it happens about three weeks before being forced to fly and the thought of a poor moggy being homeless is the last straw for the traumatised owner.

In tender moments I have been known to offer to cat sit, or dog sit while the owners go on leave. But never again will I rabbit sit. Not since I discovered that Flopsy, the long-eared rabbit, was accustomed to doing his business through the gaps in the wooden verandah.

Then there was Pontius the parrot whose permanently departing owner successfully dumped him on a friend of mine. It wasn't until the final farewells that the ex-owner thought to inform the new owner that parrots need their own passport.

Pontius proved extremely difficult when escorted to the photo booth for both frontal and profile shots. He also nearly killed Grandma. Pontius had mastered the most ear-piercing wolf whistle, which served to terrify Grandma out of her wits in the middle of the first night of her visit to her daughter.

'I thought there was a strange man in the house,' she whispered faintly, whilst being plucked from the hall floor by a half-naked son-in-law, who had responded to the scream.

Which brings me on to quarantine. I recall so clearly the sight of Diana, newly arrived in Norway. She brought a gathering of forty expatriate women close to tears, when she gave a heart-rending presentation on the unfairness of the dog import laws. Her trick was to vividly describe her wonderful labrador and then to dramatically wield her empty dog basket round and round her head.

If anyone did not deserve a hard time, it was Peter. He had been such a good friend in offering to cat sit while his friends went away on holiday. Little did he know that the cat would decide to take out every bit of venom in his might on Peter for being the unquestionable cause of his real parents taking flight. Those of you who know cats might say that this is par for the course. I agree, nothing unusual about that. Nor was it perhaps unusual that Peter had strict instructions to keep the cat flap open at all times. The real parents however, were perhaps unaware how little Peter knew about cats and how unfamiliar and unrecogniz-able they were to him. So when Peter came in to feed the cat one morning, he was appalled

'You should have seen the state the place was in. It looked as if a whirlwind had raged around the place for days, and it had only been overnight. Do you know what I'd done? I'd let the wrong cat in the kitchen and fed it, and it didn't know the way out of course. So there was the wrong cat inside, running amok and the real cat outside, too frightened to come in. I can tell you, I'll never look after anyone's cat again!'

Let that be a lesson to all us cat-lovers – make sure your carer knows your cat!

In many countries wild or stray dogs and cats can be a menace. Children, however, fall in love with them and beg their parents to let them stay. Know the story? Once wild always wild I'm afraid.

I know of Helen in Dubai, who refused to tolerate the constant screeches of a cat that mewed plaintively and constantly outside her door. Her husband let it in and fed it, insisting that Biggles, as he became known, would calm down in time. Like his relative the leopard he neither changed his spots nor his screaming. Eventually the housegirl took pity and, without telling a soul, smuggled Biggles into a carrier bag, took him to the other side of the Creek and left him there. She looked smug for weeks before finally admitting her deed to a calmer Helen, when she asked for the taxi money.

Dogs, like cars, come second-hand in expatriate circles. It is not always a bad thing to be able to adopt a road tested and house trained pet to play with your children. The trouble is that second-hand canines just do not understand that their previous owners have moved on. I heard of Masafi from Muscat who would leap the garden fence and trot gaily down the centre of the main road back to her original home. There she would dolefully and hopefully look into the eyes of the complete stranger who now occupied her real home. Then just as her wan-derlust was calmed, and the new owners had raised the fence, they too were posted.

Although expat pets, in themselves, are no different from any other tame ani-mals, I really think it's time we had a word with their owners, don't you?

This is the World Service
by Mark Eadie, English in The Sultanate of Oman
The lengths we go to for the football results.

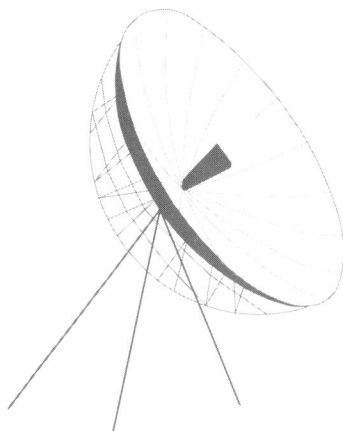

In times of trouble, television and radio stations seem to consider it necessary to play martial music. Madagascar was different. In 1991, with a national strike and constant threats of a coup, the national television station played endless videos of an American gospel choir. Each night it was the same choir beating out the same message of salvation and joy. It was a particularly odd choice as less than one Malagasy in a thousand speaks any English at all.

Living away from the reaches of terrestrial and satellite television for nine months, even the gospel singers didn't make it to Miandrivazo, 200 km south west of the capital. I was forced to rely on the BBC World Service for news and entertainment, just as my parents had done in Cyprus back in the 60's. Little seems to have changed since then at Broadcasting House.

The BBC World Service forces your imagination into overtime: it is simply not possible to have the Beeb, as she is affectionately known, on in the background. You have to concentrate to hear what is being said or sung. The famous hiss and crackle, and the occasional flash of Chinese or Russian interference makes it a difficult task. The radio becomes the focal part of the room.

The news, on the hour, every hour, is still read in a dry, monotonous voice. It is easy to imagine the newsreader in some darkened room in Regent's Street recalling the day's atrocities into an enormous microphone. For some reason, I always picture the newsreader wearing a suit and tie. In reality, they are probably wearing jeans and a tee shirt.

Plays are still read into the stratosphere on a regular basis. Who listens to these monologues, crackling and hissing into the still tropical air? My mind's eye tells me it will be a planter in Papua New Guinea, a retired civil servant in Simla, or a logger in Bolivia. I just cannot imagine today's development workers, oilfield technicians, or diplomats settling down with a glass of scotch to tune into Under Milk Wood.

Listening to the World Service is indeed a labour of love. Seemingly, wherever one lives, reception is poor: too much concrete or too much mountain interference. The key to good reception is a good aerial. The house of a seasoned World Service listener can be recognised instantly by the wires running obtrusively across the sitting room wall, through a tangle of sweetheart vines, out of the window and up to the roof. Fifteen metres of copper cable and fancy connections are a testimony to the hours spent on hiss-reduction. It seems that all efforts are in vain, for the important words are always turned to hiss, as if a censor with a serious sense of humour failure is working overtime in West London. In fact I'm convinced the hiss is injected at source to give authenticity. If not, then can you explain why I always receive Radio Vietnam perfectly?

While working in one of Madagscar's more remote areas, Saturday evenings saw me 30 km from base, on the top of a mountain, sitting on the roof of the trusty Land Cruiser, with the aerial of my Sony pointed vaguely at the Seychelles. The second-half commentary of a Premiership match always transports me back home, to the terraces of cold feet, steaming hot pies and Bovril. Trying to explain all this to the platoon of infantry, who caught me there one evening, was remarkably difficult. Even the disembodied cheers, as Nottingham Forest scored a late equaliser, failed to impress them: they were sure I was a spy. It took two hours at the Miandrivazo police station to convince them.

For our four years, in Oman, modern technology has reduced the importance of the World Service, but not completely. I now get the football results courtesy of Compuserve, but on a Saturday evening, you can still find me hanging off the balcony, pointing the aerial vaguely in the direction of The Seychelles.

I wish Radio Vietnam carried the Premiership results.

In the Halo Halo Bar
by Janet Olearski, English in The Philippines
Some customs are hard to swallow.

I was in Iloilo City – Ilo ilo – and was being persuaded, against my better judgement, to try halo halo. They'd heard I liked ice cream. It was true.

To try this amazing dish you have to go to a sort of Filipino fast food bar. You pay for your halo halo and you're presented with a large sundae dish. You proceed to a table, which is loaded with a variety of multicoloured food items: jackfruit, corn, fried banana, green shiny cubes of gelatine, red jelly beans, flakes of almond, small brown beans, slimy shreds of coconut. These are just a few of the delicacies to choose from when you prepare your personalised halo halo. You load them into the bottom of your dish, adding sugar if you wish – though everything is already heavily sweetened. Then you pack the lot in tightly with several layers of crushed ice, pour a teapot of condensed milk over it and crown it all with huge scoops of purple ice cream.

When I had finished preparing mine there was a queue of people behind me, all standing patiently with empty dishes, waiting in silence to have second helpings. I noticed that they only took the ice cream.

A sign above the table invites you to eat as much as you like and to 'be fair, don't share.' You can go back for more yourself, but may not hand your dish over to a non-paying friend.

We sat upstairs in a window seat, watching the Iloilo City traffic pass by. Except for the jeepneys and the beaten up cabs I could have been in Notting Hill Gate. A television played in the main dining area, suspended from the ceiling like in an airport. The tables were glossy, plastic and bolted to the floor. In the background, above the general hubbub, a voice announced garbled messages over the loudspeaker system. Numbers were called and people got up and went downstairs to collect their food. I noticed they weren't eating halo halo. After a few mouthfuls of mine, neither was I.

Money Worries

by Paul Cleary, English in Europe

Whoever said expatriates had no money worries?

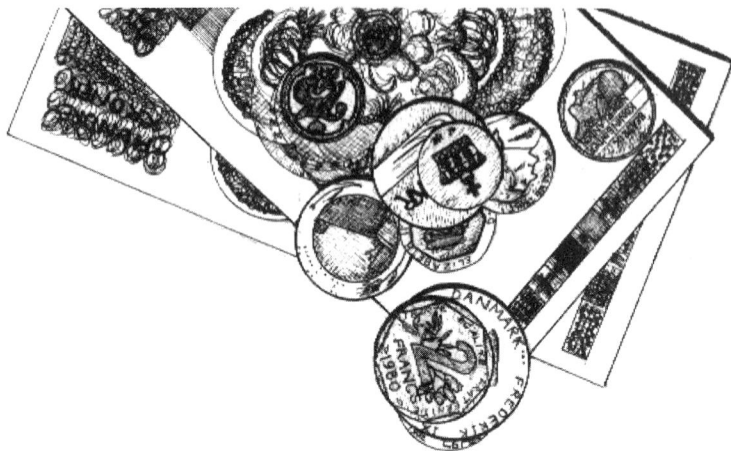

I wouldn't say Norway was expensive. Well, I might ... if you paid me. I guess it depends what you compare it with. Compared to Tokyo it's cheap. Here in Norway VAT is 23 per cent, beer is almost five quid a pint and we can hardly bear to talk about the cost of a new car. But why? Partly geographical – long country, lots of mountains, tough climate. Partly political – refuse to join Europe, expensive imports. Partly economics – some people (present company excepted) get paid too much. And when you have too much money chasing too few goods you get inflation. They say inflation is virtually non-existent here but fail to let on that they put the highest duties on anything that smacks of luxury - petrol, alcohol, tobacco.

There are two theories as to why the government slaps so many taxes on things. The first is that they need the money, which is questionable. The second is that they are trying to stop everyone from enjoying themselves.

The frightening thing about living here is that you get used to the prices. It is only when you next go abroad that you realise you have been paying far too much. So, the next time you find yourself in the Duty Free Shop at Terminal 3 at Heathrow, take a look around. If you see a chap staggering down the aisle resembling a mobile off-licence, stand behind him and look at his boarding card. Chances are he's heading for Scandinavia, where gin normally retails at £28 a bottle. On the plane he will not be bashful in availing himself of the complimentary drinks. I've seen terrified stewardesses abandon their trolleys in the middle of the business section rather than suffer the barrage of orders.

I spent half of my adult life in Switzerland, where the bank teller sits behind bazooka-proof glass, stretching from floor to ceiling. He talks to you through a microphone and hands you the money via a turntable. Notes are counted by machine, always in pristine condition and virtually untouched by human hand. When I first arrived there, interest rates were negative. You paid the bank for the privilege of keeping your money there.

In Norway, the bank counter is waist high and piles of readies lie around in full view. One athletic gate vault and you'd be sitting on the cashier's lap. They count the notes by wearing sawn-off condoms on one hand. These must be periodically moistened with spittle. I have sometimes been handed objects which bear more resemblance to the Dead Sea Scroll than a 100 kroner note. Having said all this, Norway's electronic payment systems are among the most modern in the world and Norwegians are rapidly heading towards a cashless society here. Cheques disappeared years ago and they are seriously into telephone and PC banking. Plastic magic is very much in evidence.

Talking of which, one of the problems of living abroad so long is that the English language changes while you are away. New words are added (I heard my first 'bog standard' when last there) and old words take on new meanings. Apparently 'bad' now means 'good'. Anyway, during a recent visit, I was trying to pay by credit card in a London shop. They had one of those little machines on the counter that reads the magnetic stripe, checks your creditworthiness, debits your account and tells your fortune.

The shop assistant told me to 'swipe' my card. Having left England a quarter of a century earlier I was still under the impression that 'swipe' meant to 'hit' or 'steal'. I must have looked 'gobsmacked' (first used in England in 1975, I'm told). I could not understand why the assistant should expect me to walk off without paying and waited for her to say 'Just joking, Sir.' She didn't. In fact she said it again: 'You have to swipe it.'

So there we stood, strangers in our own country. A pimply adolescent waiting behind me came to my rescue. He raised his eyes to the ceiling.

'You gotta swipe it... look like this.' He gesticulated over the machine with his own card.

'I say, you must think I'm awfully stupid,' I gurgled embarrassingly. 'I've been away a long time you know.'

'Obviously not long enough,' I heard the shop assistant mumble under her breath.

The Execu-Wife Elucidates
by Christine Yates, English in Germany
It's a job being married to a high-flying expatriate executive.

Your husband saw the ad . . .

'Dynamic, hands-on sales oriented MD needed to take division of US multinational corporation into the next century. Location: Overseas.'

He applied and after an age of meetings, hesitation and yet more meetings, signed up. You wait and see ... then give up your career, swap the furniture, let the house and say farewell to your social life, friends, family, lifestyle and, finally, with a certain amount of anguish, surrender control over your destiny. You become a Dependent, or, in the eyes of the Corporation, a chattel.

I bet that in a drawer of every Human Resources Director in every American multinational corporation there sits a 'Confidential' file with the job description for Execu-wife paper-clipped to a photo of Princess Diana. It is, in computer-speak a virtual role, one that in theory exists, but never actually appears, like Godot himself.

Which also explains why most of the senior executives of the Corporation treat you like a spoilt, pretty but empty-headed child; polite enough just in case you may have to exist and patronising enough for you to recognise your place in the patriarchy that is corporate America!

The advertisement for such a position, politically correct, might read something like this:

> Young, dynamic MD of international business headquartered in Germany and America seeks a high-calibre Executive Assistant. Must be multi-talented and an excellent organiser with patience, a sense of humour and a pragmatic approach to business. You will co-ordinate his business and personal lives and attend high-level meetings. There will be plenty of opportunity to take on and run your own projects. You must be calm under pressure and have strong interpersonal skills. The challenges are many and will test your intellectual and social skills to the limit. Package wholly negotiable for the right person. *Call Jekyll & Hyde Associates.*

What the Execu-wife would see is this:

Headquartered in Germany and America
The Lufthansa air hostesses will see more of your husband than you will!

A high-calibre Executive Assistant
Companion, cook, helpmeet, confidante, partner and personal factotum who can speak easily with shareholders, Chief Executives, secretaries or salesmen, in three languages, sober or drunk!

Must be multi-talented
Housewife, luggage-packer, hostess, travelling companion, nose-wiper, walking Encyclopaedia, restaurant guide, linguist, entertainer, sex kitten and stray sock finder.

An excellent organiser with patience, a sense of humour and a pragmatic approach to business
Don't be fooled by this collection of virtues. This means that you must have the nouse to acknowledge that whilst you may be operating in an egalitarian, post-feminist New Man marital partnership, the Corporation will have a Stone Age view of women, often referred to collectively as The Wives, like in Stepford, and, I suspect, with the same objective. The Corporation will therefore expect utter humility, self-abasement and unquestioning hero-worship when you are allowed to meet any of its executives – unless, of course, you happen to be taller than them, in which case, bad luck! Slouching is unacceptable, flat shoes are dowdy and on top of that, it is bad form to draw the attention of those vertically-challenged executives, whose hairdresser only should be allowed intimate knowledge of their thinning crown, to your un-Stone Age height.

You will co-ordinate his business and personal lives
Displaying Moony-like devotion when yet again your personal plans are wrecked by another corporate event and pausing only to reapply your mascara as unhesitatingly you move your life and Hoover bag contents across Europe. By the way, never expect this Corporation to know anything about a country where the dollar is not the currency, other than it is foreign and the natives are not to be trusted.

Attend high-level meetings
Where your 'shakehand-and-greeting' skills (110/55) will be used with regular, though not royal, frequency.

Have plenty of opportunity to take on your own projects
Like joining an expatriate wives club and finding, in a state of utter bewilderment, that you have agreed to host, in your own home, tasteless make-up demonstra-

tions for pyramid sellers whose sales techniques make grave robbers seem subtle and whose make-up know-how apes Tutankamun's. Moreover, as a Committee member (how did that happen?) you will be required to hold a c-c-c-c-coffee morning, thereby allowing the most critical and vocal analysts of Western domestic interior taste into your own home.

You must be calm under pressure and have strong interpersonal skills

Above all, a sense of the ridiculous is paramount, coupled with the ability to sit like 'Patience on a monument smiling at grief' or at whichever fashionably anorexic doll-woman you happen to sit opposite at dinner. This can be quite fun – watching a stick-thin American trophy-wife trying to eat a light meal of fish, steamed vegetables and salad without having to chew, swallow or digest any of it is a wonder of modern civilisation. There is real art!

The challenges will test your intellectual and social skills to the limit

Because if you don't keep a perspective you will go mad or suddenly take to wearing loon pants and purple eyeshadow again. Moreover, don't expect that what you have achieved in your own right will count for anything with the Corporation, where your mere existence as a 'wife' causes them expense. Much better if executives are single or even discreetly gay.

Package wholly negotiable for the right person

Including major health insurance - you hope!

Call Jekyll & Hyde Associates

Beware of a firm with a name like this. Always check them out by taking a number and calling them back!

The Expat Husband
by Susan Ventris, English in Norway
When your husband is no longer the man you married.

Back home, my husband was a pretty ordinary kind of chap. During the week, he worked at the office, and watched television in the evenings. At weekends, he searched B&Q for paintstripper and applied weedkiller to the garden. His idea of excitement was a trip to Homebase to look for a patio set. The most challenging thing that ever happened to him was when the DIY shop ran out of cornflower blue emulsion. You always knew where he was, in those days.

And then we were posted overseas.

Suddenly, we found ourselves living in a rented house where all our needs were taken care of. If anything went wrong around the house, we made a phone call. Nature abhors a vacuum, and so did my husband. All that pent-up energy that used to be channelled into decorating had to be used up somehow. Like many male expatriates he channelled it into sport. Rumour has it that there are men who channel their energy elsewhere. They are material for another article no doubt, but I'm not going to be the one to write it.

Not just any sport, of course. A gentle putt putt around a tennis court does nothing for the male ego. Men are naturally drawn to unusual and dangerous sports, and, by a quirk of nature, the more out of condition they are, the more death-defying the sport they tend to choose. And living abroad opens up a whole new field of sporting endeavour for the newly liberated husband. I've known husbands who've taken up bungie-jumping, and husbands who've gone off white-water rafting. Fortunately, I haven't been married to them. My husband chose skiing, a sport that was entirely new to him.

Now I have nothing against skiing. It's a fine sport. My husband assured me that he was in the peak of athletic condition, and who was I to argue? I knew that he was flexible because I'd witnessed the contortions he got into painting the hall ceiling. All those sprints across the living-room to fetch the remote control for the television must have built up stamina, and everyone knows that beer is a fine body-building material. Nevertheless, I decided to err on the side of caution and took myself off to England rather than be witness to his maiden voyage on skis.

It would not be an exaggeration to say that he sank before leaving the harbour. The exertion of putting on his ski-boots proved a little too taxing. Bending down, he experienced a sharp spasm in his back. Not wishing to appear weak in front of his Norwegian friends, all of whom had been skiing since they were in romper suits, he gamely skied for the rest of the day. Nature finally caught up with him when the party stopped at a café on the way home. Rising out of his chair, he experienced a further spasm as his back locked. Emitting an anguished cry of pain and humiliation, he sank to his knees. A small crowd gathered around him. In a spectacle that witnesses have described as profoundly moving, yet faintly hilarious, he was carried out to the car and driven home.

Back home his condition worsened. He crawled to the phone to request the aid of our nearest (male) neighbour. His friend cooked tea for our daughter and summoned medical assistance. The doctor arrived to discover my husband laid out on the floor complaining of back pain while his friend shuffled around the kitchen in a pinny. This is the sort of behaviour that tends to get you a reputation in a small town. I can't help thinking that none of this would have happened if we'd stayed at home.

And then there are the financial problems. Back home, our major financial decision was whether to pay the gas bill promptly, or wait until they got really nasty. A decision my husband was quite happy to leave to me. Suddenly, he found himself earning a salary the size of the national debt of a small country. For the first time, he got interested in money.

Nowadays, our home is visited regularly by the sort of people you'd normally cross the street to avoid. Insurance salesmen. Financial advisors. They slap him on the back and call him by his first name. They know more about us than our mothers do, and what's more, it's all down in writing. Forms. We've filled out hundreds of them. Forms for policies we're not even interested in, forms for schemes we haven't a hope of understanding even if we devote the rest of our lives to studying financial matters.

Not that I'm complaining. At least if something goes wrong you have someone to sue if you take financial advice. It was when my husband decided to play the stock market that things got really worrying. Expatriate men like to do that. It gives them something to talk about when they can't get about because of their injuries. He has it fifty percent right anyway. He knows exactly how to buy shares. He's a dab hand at buying. It's just the how and when to sell that seems to be causing problems.

Expatriate husbands are a funny breed. They're in the unique postion of being able to fulfil their boyhood ambitions. This may not be a popular theory with the male sex, but it's arguable that most young men have fairly straightforward ambitions. They want to drive powerful cars, play loud musical instruments and travel to wacky places to perform improbably athletic feats. (There may be a few who long to devote their lives to spiritual development or services to mankind, but I've never met any). Mercifully, most men are restricted by financial obligations from fulfilling their boyhood dreams. They settle down to domesticity, where their daily habits are as predictable as the phases of the moon, and about as exciting.

Not the expatriate man, however. Given a hefty salary and undreamt of opportunities to travel, the expatriate is in a position to drink long and deep from the well of life, though some prefer to do so from a whisky bottle. Overseas, you become aware of new aspects of your husband's personality, not all of which belong to the man you married.

Even the summer holidays are a dangerous time. A time when many wives take the children back to visit their mother, rather than his. A time when husbands are never able to extend their holiday that little bit further. They wave goodbye so sadly at the departure gate and you tell them to take care. But the moment they're home alone it's a different story. Somehow they never find the time to hoover the carpet or water the plants. Neither do they summon up the energy to defrost and reheat all those carefully prepared meals for one, that you laboured over in the last weeks of the school term. Instead they feast on fast food and only telephone at three in the morning to tell you about a particularly wild evening with the boys.

One friend of mine told of the queues of wifefree expatriate husbands in the doctor's surgery, all waiting to have their ear plugs removed. When the wife's away the boys really start to play.

The real trouble begins when they expect you to join them in their pursuits. I should know. I'm the sort of quiet soul who likes nothing better than to spend the evening reading Jane Austen. I like to play soothing classical music on the piano. Then my husband got his drum kit – an event he could never have hoped for in our semi back home. Loud and drunken males appeared in our basement, equipped with electric guitars and amplifiers. I found myself mysteriously propelled towards a keyboard and instructed to 'just play a few chords'. That was four years ago and I'm still playing the same chords.

My Friend Godzilla
by Phyllis Adler, American in England
When your husband turns into an animal.

The door opens, the sound of a suitcase thuds to the floor . . . Your life is about to change: your partner is returning from a business trip.
Usually, it is my husband who has been away and I have been at home with the children. While he has been gone, the tone of the house has altered. I operated with less structure and on a more equal basis with my teenage children. There was debate and we aimed for democratic decision. Calm has reigned.

Then in waltzes Godzilla*!

Like any wary animal, Godzilla immediately senses the change in the atmosphere of his cave. He sniffs the air and looks about him. Godzilla reacts quickly to uneasy feelings of displacement. In order to re-establish his place by the hearth, he closely questions everyone on the issues of the week. We had all been quite proud of the methods we had used to head off our crises, but no, we soon discover how remiss we have been. Various inadequacies are pointed out plainly and blunty. We are made to feel like failures in self-management. And if anyone knows about management, it is Godzilla. After all he has been on a business trip to another country, battled with natives and survived unscathed. While we have merely had to deal with leaky taps and unprogrammable video recorders.

This is not exactly the welcome home by candlelight I envisioned during his absence. After five minutes of scrutiny, I wonder who it is exactly that I thought I was missing.

What is happening is not

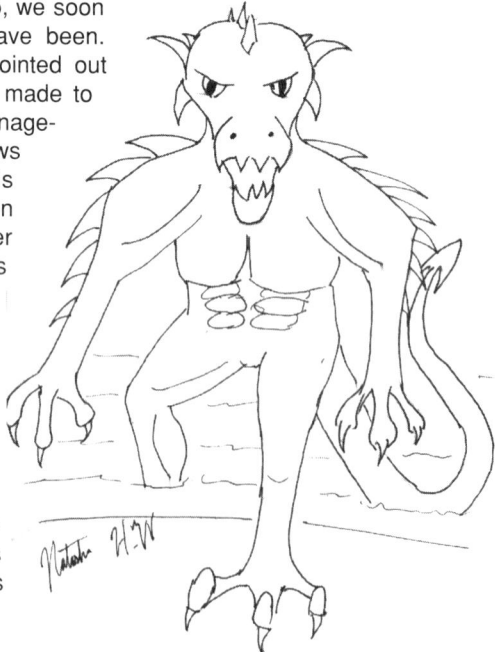

dissimilar to the territorial impulses we see acted out before us every day on CNN. It is simply a microcosmic example combined with the stress from the trip. Add to that the God-like symptoms that develop in those on the company expense account. This person, who has been feeling super-human in some ways, and – hopefully – a bit lonely in others, enters his lair. He is eager to become part of the whole again. But unfortunately he has not had time to set aside the 'work-week' mode of operation and re-adjust to kitchen customs.

In my own home, this process of mini culture-shock and territoriality plays itself out in a fairly traditional setting. Currently, I do not have an office outside the home. But what if there are two of you regularly coming and going and frequently re-establishing and re-asserting territorial needs? The effects can be very hazardous, both to your marriage and your health.

When we were younger, the re-entry time for my travelling hubby was much longer than it is now. Sometimes, these days, it is down to nine not-so-easy-to-live-with minutes. At least, as with all things that you have experienced before, you develop a sure knowledge that it will pass. In the beginning of our life together, I didn't have the distance or the goodwill to realise that in large measure, with this person, it was mostly a need to be in the heart of the family again that prompted this carnage. And it took many well-chosen moments to gently let my buddy know this re-entry behaviour was not going to fly, even though he did.

Twenty six years on, we are still ironing out the kinks.

I have found comfort in knowing that this scene is not unique. Unfortunately, travelling marriages do not always reflect us at our best. Every time a plane lands, someone, somewhere will behave in this totally normal, if not enjoyable, manner. In the home, as on CNN, we are more primitive than we like to admit. Just ask my friend, Godzilla!

Printed with permission of Godzilla.
Reprinted with permission of Dual Career Network magazine.

Another Suitcase Another Long Haul

by Peter Gosling, an Expatriate Visitor

When your daughter only loves you for your luggage allowance.

'I'm going to get married,' our daughter suddenly announced.

Sighs of relief all round. We thought he was never going to ask her.

'And we're going to live abroad.'

'Where?' we asked, our jaws dropping.

"It's in the Gulf,' she explained. 'Look, I'll show you.'

She opened the atlas and pointed to a place that was a black dot in the middle of a vast sandy coloured area. It seemed one heck of a way from England.

'You'll be able to visit us,' she said seeing that our faces had assumed a look of terror at the thought of our little girl being trapped in an oasis surrounded by camels.

'It's really quite civilized,' she explained patiently. 'They have shops, proper houses and an airport.'

And so it was that a few months after the frantic arrangements for the wedding and the tearful farewells, the call came.

'We've got a nice flat and there's a spare room for you. Do come, you'll love it. And by the way could you bring ... ?'

That was the start of the lists that were going to dominate our lives for the next few years. At first it was just a few of the wedding presents that had taken up residence in our garage. Oh, and could we possibly cram some of her favourite tea in our case, and a couple of pork pies (impossible to get out there) and her Cliff Richard tapes.

Suitably loaded we set off and I must admit that what we experienced when we got there was nothing like our expectations. We were welcomed into the arms of their new friends and whisked off to beach clubs, fed in exciting ethnic restaurants and introduced to the magic of a barbecue at night in the desert.

Having developed a taste for the expat life we found that we were doing the trip twice a year and enjoying every new experience. Christmas Day on the beach in swimwear was certainly different from crouching over a fire watching re-runs of the Morecambe and Wise Christmas Show. The turkey and all the bits were familiar, but acquired a different character when served on a verandah hung about with bougainvillea.

Of course, each trip was accompanied by the inevitable request list, sewing machine, food mixer and the usual supply of foodstuffs unobtainable in the local supermarkets. There were times, indeed, when we seriously considered hiring our own cargo jet. But then along came the grandchildren. Or rather, the first grandchild closely followed by the second. Now our list of goodies to bring became longer and far more complex. Soon we came to consider ourselves as a combination of the Royal Logistical Corps and Oxfam. Children's medicines featured high on the list, followed by a selection of the products of that well-known chain store that supplies Lady Thatcher's undies. Still, we never minded heaving two trolleys of luggage across the departure hall at Heathrow. Very often, when I was so worried about our luggage being overweight , I was expecting to make the flight wearing two pairs of trousers and three shirts.

These were happy years despite the struggle with bulging suitcases and long night flights, for our time as honorary expats has come to an end. Our son-in-law now has a job in England and they are coming back to live in their own house in the village next to us. Things will never be the same, but I shall still have that uncontrollable urge to stuff a case with food parcels and announce that we're coming to stay for a month.

Rain, Rain Go Away
by Terri Nagel, American in Norway
Rain reigns in Stavanger.

We live in a rainy part of the world. To clarify this even further, we live in a rainy, cold part of the world. Winter here lasts ten months. The rain, however, lasts a full 12 months of the year. This is no joke. There is no spring. One morning we wake up and summer has magically appeared.

Because we live in Europe, along one of the coastal cities, we get the 'wonderful' effects of the North Sea. The temperature here is moderate. We rarely get below 0 degrees celsius. It hovers at this mark, however, for many months. I'm not sure that 12 months of rain is worth this temperate climate.

My husband accepted a temporary transfer here in October of 93. We've lived here three years now and still have another two years to go. Like any assignment, the years go by both quickly and slowly. A lot of it has to do with the weather.

Having lived in the Chicago area our entire lives, you would think our family is used to this. We're not. Neal and I have been married 13 years now and, like most employees working for oil companies, the majority of those assignments have been spent in warm, dry climates.

We have four children...four muddy children. Like all good Americans, our children play baseball. Have you ever seen a bunch of American kids, out on the baseball field, playing in the rain? It's not a pretty sight. The kids are issued uniforms at the beginning of the year. They're so excited. So are the parents. That excitement quickly fades as we realize that we'll never see the uniforms. We learn to recognize our kids pretty quickly by their outer wear. Between coats, hats and mittens, you hope you can decipher who's who and, better yet, you hope and pray that another child on the team doesn't have the same wellies as your child.

The baseball season itself is a sight to behold. Because the majority of the Americans are expatriates, the baseball season is played in the Spring. Spring by the calendar that is. Winter is still going strong. It took me three seasons to appreciate baseball again, as long as I have on my long-johns, my hat, my mittens, and a cup of hot chocolate firmly in hand. My oldest son, however, is embarrassed about this. He made some snide remark about my hat the other day. Apparently he would rather see his mother with bright red ears than in some dorky hat.

That of course, leads to the next topic. Mud. Lots and lots of it. I've never seen as much before moving here. My carpets are permanently soiled. I rent a carpet cleaner as often as I vacuum, which is not cheap in Norway.

After we return home from the baseball field, the kids strip their clothes, they shed their mittens and their hats. These things don't magically appear clean in time for the next game, you know. They generally don't even make it to the hamper without a lot of nagging. Only after some serious threatening, do they eventually make it to the laundry room..have you ever seen the size of the washing machines and the dryers in Europe? I'll give you a clue. They are about one third of the size of my laundry basket.

To top that off, each load takes somewhere in the vicinity of an hour and a half to two hours. Oh yes, I can do a quick load in 20 minutes. I just have to wash the clothes in cold water. Fine. Only mud stains don't come out in cold water. Remember there are six in our family? Well, I can do about two person's clothes in one load. If your multiplication is on the ball you can work out how long it takes me to do the laundry. And that's just the washing part of it.

The dryer is as bad. It is about the size of a pea. And to give you an idea of just how brain-dead this vacuuming, carpet-cleaning, laundry lady is, would you believe that I only just realised that the 120 setting on the dryer meant two hours? What's worse is that it took me two years to do the math.

After 18 months of cloud cover we took our first trip to the island of Tenerife. Pure paradise. While strolling the promenade at night, our six year old looked up at the moon and solemnly questioned what it was. I had forgotten that not only had our days been sunless for so long, but that our nights had been moonless too.

The light is now at the end of the tunnel. With just 18 more months until repatriation I am trying to decide what to whine about when we are back in Chicago.

It is a woman's prerogative to complain, isn't it?

Driving Me Mad
Joanna Parfitt, English in The Middle East
Funny how it's never your fault!

My first accident in Dubai was caused when the taxi driver in front of me braked suddenly to stop for a passenger. I drove straight up his bumper.
'But he just stopped without indicating . . . ' I stammered.
'You did not keep your distance,' replied the police officer who arrived on the scene within minutes, shaking his head as he wrote out a bill for my fine and took away my driving licence.
He was right. But all the same, it hadn't really been all my fault.
That sort of thing happens every day. Many of us have arguments with kerb-stones or traffic lights and I've often reversed into a skip.
Take the time my car ground to a halt on a Muscat roundabout. In an instant a moustached policeman on a motorbike drew up alongside.
'No petrol, madam?' he asked wryly.
I feigned shock. Actually I was shocked. I had been oblivious to the bright orange dashboard light that had accompanied me all morning.
'Sorry,' I whimpered.
'Pull over,' he commanded.
'But I can't,' I protested.
He hurrumphed.
I think he was more annoyed at my stupidity than at himself for forgetting that a car will not move without petrol.
Another police car drew up and two burly men pushed me onto a triangular traffic island before telling me to go forth and find petrol.
'Big problem,' said my moustached friend, who shook his head, grinned, hopped on his bike and disappeared. It was 100°F. I was on the way to fetch my son from school and had a boot full of gently steaming fresh fish. He was right about the problem.
Fortunately my helpless expression must have worked. A passing motorist drove me to the nearest petrol station to fill an over-priced empty water bottle with four star. The day, my waiting son and the red snapper were to be saved after all. I stood, fumbled and sweated for ten minutes until I discovered that the petrol cap on a Range Rover may not be removed unless the whole car is unlocked too. After eight years in the Middle East I had never had the need to put petrol in the

car myself. I was used to merely lowering the window and handing both keys and cash to the attendant.

It can only have been another five minutes before I was able to jump back in, mop up my blushes with an inadequate tissue and drive off the traffic island.

In a split second another policeman, though I could not actually swear he was different, flagged me down.

'Big problem madam,' he began as he drew an elaborate sketch of a car doing a U turn at the entrance to a roundabout and driving straight over the middle of the island.

'But you put me on the island,' I explained.

'Me?' he asked puzzled.

'Well one of you,' I replied, 'a policeman, two actually, put me on the island. I had run out of petrol.'

'Big problem,' he grinned then calmly rode to the middle of the road and stopped the traffic so that I could proceed.

But amusing anecdotes aside, and we all collect plenty of them, there is a very serious side to driving in the Middle East and you soon learn to drive defensively. You anticipate that people will leap out at you from junctions. You expect to be carved up, undertaken or hooted at for no apparent reason. It is nothing to find another car facing you on a roundabout or to screech to a halt when an articulated lorry pulls out to block the road.

You just grit your teeth, start to use all your mirrors for the first time since your driving test, and develop a swivel neck mechanism that an owl would be proud of. You learn to think with your hands, head and feet all at once, to administer Smarties and reprimands while negotiating potential hazards every day.

But now and again you can't take it any more. When one more person fails to give way and you are inches from disaster you can lose your cool. You toot loudly at someone who is quite blatantly in the wrong. The culprit toots back and shakes his fist. You shake yours back and point an index finger to your brain. Then he signals for you to slow down and talk it through like adults.

This brings to mind an incident, not so long ago, when my husband found himself embroiled in a similar semaphore argument.

Just as one of the kids piped up 'what's happening Daddy?', Daddy was overtaking on a blind stretch of road, leaping two feet over a speed bump and turning sharp right, then left, then right again.

'A nasty man's chasing me,' Daddy answered, juggling the gears and steering wheel with amazing dexterity as sweat dripped from his brow.

'But we don't live here, Daddy.'

In two minutes Daddy was crouched low on the floor at the back of the car, I moved into the driving seat, placed a child in a car seat in the front beside me, and hoped my long blonde hair would put our pursuer off the scent.

'What are you doing, Daddy? queried Sam.

'Nothing,' said Daddy.

Stick it Out
by Carol Mackenzie, Scottish in Norway
The blind leading the blind.

After seven years of being driven around Bangkok and Jakarta, sharing a car and driver with my husband, what a relief it was to find myself in Norway, with my very own brand new car. Admittedly, we had to cash in the life insurance policies to afford it, and the wheel seemed to be on the wrong side. Still, it was a small price to pay for the freedom to stop at as many shops as I liked without feeling feeble. It was bliss to be able to sing along to my favourite songs too.

As long as the road was straight and had some other cars on it, keeping to the right proved quite simple. Foolishly, I started to relax. Then I encountered an unfamiliar road sign – a yellow diamond on a white background. Of course, I now understand that it means cars entering a main road from a minor road to the right have the absolute authority to cut in front of you without even a glance in your direction. The brakes in new cars are pretty sharp, thankfully.

Norwegians are fit. Even pensioners sprint – onto zebra crossings cunningly concealed in front of junctions or around corners. My three year old daughter loves the excitement.

'Can you do that again Mummy?' she calls from the back seat.

I regain my composure and re-start the ignition.

Roundabouts are a bit of a gamble. The trick seems to be to keep everyone guessing. Indicators must not be allowed to give the game away. Look as if you are going straight on and then suddenly shoot round to the left, scoring points off the driver who was about to enter the roundabout. Once you've mastered this technique you can move onto shooting onto the roundabout, thus forcing the car already on it to slow down. Double points if it actually has to stop. It's a lot of fun and I think it reflects the egalitarian outlook of the locals.

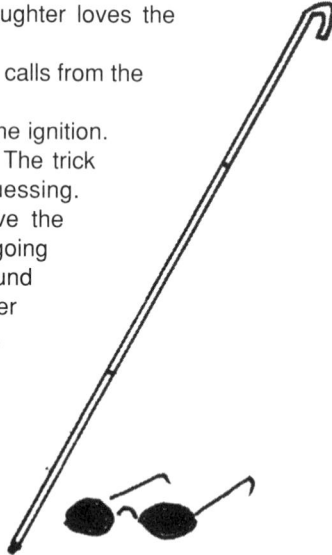

The traffic police are very visible. I keep wondering if it's guilt from a former life that washes over me whenever I see a policeman or customs official. The first time I was stopped I was driving a car from my husband's office. Was there a red triangle in the boot? Was there any paperwork in the glove box? Did I have my driving licence? It was a bit of a letdown when he only wanted to check if I was wearing my seatbelt.

The second time I was sure I was about to be given a hefty fine for exceeding the exceedingly slow speed limit. Wrong again.

The third time came after dinner with my husband and my parents and a glass of white wine. The traffic slowed down. A road block had been set up. My mind filled with terror. I had visions of getting up at 5am in the freezing cold to layer my daughter in snowsuits and fur-lined boots to catch three different buses to get her to pre-school. The shame of losing my licence and being sent to prison in front of my parents was enormous. Winding down the window, I felt as if I'd drunk the whole bottle. Of course, the traffic policeman spoke perfect English as he handed over what looked like a mobile phone and asked me to blow. I blew. I blew again. A green light came on and he told me I could drive on. I did, vowing never to drink again, not even in the safety and privacy of my own home. In Norway they test at the same time as the morning school run.

Winter came and everyone started talking knowledgeably about winter tyres. I had images of chains wrapped around the wheels of my car. Eventually I forced myself to go and get fitted with some *pigg dekk*. The hunky salesman who'd sold us the car asked me to 'just drive on the ramps'. I gulped nonchalantly and got on with it. Mercifully, I succeeded and immediately panicked about how I'd get off the ramps with the studded tyres in place, never having driven a tank before. The studs looked like hundreds of silver pinheads.

After just a week in Norway, my daughter started pre-school. I set off in good time to pick her up on her first day. I spotted an old man in the distance and made a mental note to watch out for him crossing the road. As I approached, he stuck a white stick out in front of my car. Instinctively I slowed down, wondering if he needed assistance. In what seemed like a flash he'd opened the passenger door, climbed in and handed me a holdall. I looked down at the holdall in my lap and across at the blind old man talking to me. He seemed to be stringing lots of consonants together without the presence of a single vowel. Suddenly it dawned on me that not everyone speaks English. I hadn't started my Norwegian class yet. He continued rambling and out of the wilderness of sound I recognised the name of a local shopping centre. Off we went and I deposited him and his holdall at the door and sped off to greet Amy – on time. A few weeks later I picked him up again and took him to the centre of town. Not that my Norwegian had improved any. He pointed the way with his stick.

Summer is here. It is hard to keep my eyes on the road with such spectacular scenery. We drive alongside a fjord, the sunroof open, Pocahontas, Amy and I blasting out *The Colours of the Wind*.

Bellydance
by Gurpreet Tirwana, English in Egypt
How it feels to drive in Cairo.

It's an elaborate dance, the body's motions fluid and snakelike to the continuous beat of the sun's drumming rays. The torso is the seething, sweating mass of traffic undulating through maze-like streets and over scrolling interconnecting bridges. The limbs and feet slink along alleys, as fingers embrace slim, dark gullies. This is Egypt's special exotic dance, performed without pausing for breath, in its belly, Cairo.

Unlike traditional Middle Eastern dancing, in my experience, this belly dance did not soothe and provide relief to my painful back. My muscles and tendons did not loosen, but ached and tightened as tension took hold of me each time I took hold of the steering wheel.

Perhaps the whole performance would be better likened to dancing techno – the jarring, stop start rhythm, pulsating through my head and penetrating my biorhythm. Even after retreating to the sanctity of my home, the beat drummed through my window frames, and cymbals and horns crashed against the panes.

On the dance floor the performers are many and varied. Jostling to get ahead are automobiles - both young and those that should have been pensioned off years ago, burly buses, intimidating lorries, annoying minibuses, frustrated taxis, boisterous motorbikes, daring cyclists, and ragged donkeys straining under the weight of overloaded carts. At tram junctions however, they are all forced to pause, to allow trams to pass languorously by. A barrier does not come down, and more vehicles than you suppose could possibly make it, speed through in front of the slowly advancing tram, risking leaving their tail bumpers on its front fender. There is no pause in the music, the chorus of impatient horns prods passengers to wake and jump off the tram at their stop.

Somehow, miraculously, the space available for the myriad vehicles is flexible, expanding horizontally and vertically to accommodate many more than promised by the width of the road. The condition of Cairo's roads varies tremendously depending on their location. Those that run through prestigious areas such as Heliopolis, home to the President, Parliament and many ministers, are velvety smooth and spotlessly clean. Driving on these roads is hazardous since every ten metres or so, there is an old man, bent double, waging his own personal war on sand and grime, armed only with a dustpan and brush. In other neighbourhoods driving hazards are presented by uneven, bumpy roads where the tarmac may be worn down to expose gaping holes of gravel.

The secret to driving successfully in Cairo is to expect outrageous and unthinkable events to happen. After all, dancing is a form of self-expression, and the blaring horns and clamorous vehicles play an ever changing tune.

As with mastering any new movement, with practise I grew bolder, and started to have fun.

Telly Addicts
Mark Eadie, English in The Netherlands
After time In Madagascar and Muscat, Mark is an expert on the telly.

It is perhaps a sad reflection of today's expatriate life that the television has become the central focus of our evening entertainment. In the last four years every house has sprouted a satellite dish. Some have two. In Europe, satellite dishes appear neat, the size of a large pan lid, strapped to the side of the house. Not so in the Middle East, where most houses have dishes that would put Jodrell Bank to shame. Huge saucers beaming down the best that Rupert Murdoch can offer.

While Star TV's dominance of the Asian satellite market is now being challenged by newer stations, it was Star that transformed television in the Middle East. Back in its heyday we would get Whose Line is it Anyway every night. Usually the same episode – but not the whole episode – just part of it – to fill in for the lack of advertising. Quickly, corporations from Melbourne to Cairo jumped on the bandwagon, and such great television soaps as *The Bold and the Beautiful* and *Santa Barbara*, appeared. Both featured characters with names as unlikely as Ridge or Thorne, who were often played by replacement actors without warning. Such classics were connected by adverts for such unlikely products as underground trains, suspension bridges and coal. Star TV made the unusual decision to make programmes fit their slots by running half-sized episodes of programmes such as The Bill and London's Burning. They never mentioned this to viewers, but even the most casual observer must have noticed that since the commercial break, the story line had completely changed.

Television, and its rapid deterioration, is a popular dinner party topic. However, I have it on good authority that the loudest critics are secretly recording Santa Barbara back home while emphatically slandering it over the chocolate mousse. In time, both Star TV and most advertisers realised that their average viewer was unlikely to be a regular consumer of underground trains. MTV soon left the dish, followed, very sadly, by the BBC World Service. A sad loss. Like the radio version, the BBC World Service offered news on the hour and we could have fun watching Michael Fish in front of a map of most of the southern hemisphere, saying 'it looks like rain in Africa tonight.'

For sports coverage Prime Sports is the standard channel and shows a huge range of sports popular with a small range of viewers. The Asians are unimpressed by beach football, wrestling or cricket sixes. The Westerners are less than riveted to the national Chinese soccer leagues. And while the commentary comes in English, the interested viewers are less than happy and the advertisers not at all.

Times look bleak for the expatriate couch potato. It is not possible to please all of the people all of the time, particularly when expatriate populations in so many Eastern areas consist of a wide mix of nationalities, most of which are not English speaking.

Global satellites bring global programming and as a result, the bland leads the bland.

Now where did I leave the remote control?

Wife at Large in Paris
Louise Rankin, English in Norway
The truth about tagging along on a free business trip

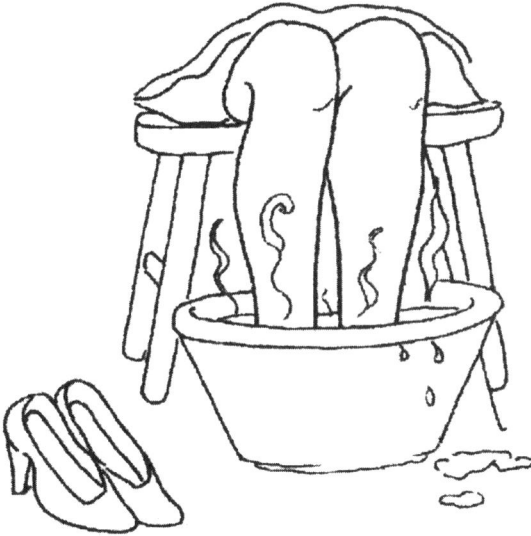

'**Is this your first time?**' said a pink-suited lady dripping with the latest home-party jewellery.

Now I wonder how she guessed? Was it my clothes? Was it my attention to the host's words? Or were the traces of insecurity stamped all over my forehead?

Actually, I consider myself quite a seasoned traveller, but yes, this was my first trip as a business man's wife and the five other ladies in the party were all in the process of sizing each other up.

'Par for the course,' I was told by a dear friend prior to departure, 'but you'll love them all by the end of it.' I had the gravest of doubts about the pink-suited version, but I tried to be open-minded at this early stage of the trip.

There we all were sitting round the breakfast table on the first morning. Several of the others had settled into eating the right sort of breakfast. There are certainly a few rules in this situation. You must never touch the bacon and eggs, for example, otherwise you will be labelled as a glutton. However, when you visibly look as if you already are a glutton, you must make a choice between confirming their opinion that this is why you got this fat in the first place, or going for the safe option by filling your plate with unfilling fruit and gain a few brownie points while they commend you for making an effort.

'Have you decided what to do today?' said a Laura Ashley dressed woman with a country-fresh face.

At that moment my own cotton frock was hanging in the bathroom trying to de-crump from its journey in the smallest suitcase I have ever been known to use. I was actually inordinately proud of the fact that I could boast to my husband that he was travelling with a lady who could, this time, pack in a smaller suit-case than his own.

I had planned to take back home the odd memento, even if he had to pack it in his suitcase, but I had a funny feeling that Per had other plans. He remem-bers well that irresistible Portuguese pottery breakfast-ware set I forced him to carry on as hand luggage. It nearly made a hole in the floor of the plane back from Lisbon as well as a hole in his pocket when he had to buy an extra holdall! I am sure it was the cause of the hostess asking some of the passengers to move to the back of the plane to balance it out .

Let's move on to the second morning breakfast. Having been shamed out of my leggings and comfy tee shirt into my crumpled frock, I was horrified to discover that Day One had obviously been the day to impress people in smart clothes. Day Two was shorts and tee shirts day.

'Oh well, at least she's trying,' I could swear I heard someone muttering in the hotel corridor.

Of the five wives, I was relieved to see that there were at least two who looked as if they might be sufferable even if one was well into her forties and was trying to be a punk model all in black, with an orange stripe in her hair. Now there were only five of us, but as soon as we went shopping it was quite clear that our differences went further than our dress size. Hooray Heidi was into classical cut glass. Punky Anne-Marie favoured spiky jewellery. Earthy Els wanted to look at recycled paper products. Sadly the Rue St Honoré was not able to serve us all.

So we moved on to the day's cultural event. Be warned: there is always one wife who tries to take over. When we gave Heidi an inch she took a mile (a Norwegian mile at that). Literally. We spent half an hour walking round all four walls of the courtyard building of the Louvre, retracing our steps twice, only to find that the way in was where we had started. Of course we had all known that in the beginning, but no-one had dared to say.

Worse was to come, because the others soon saw fit to promote me as their leader. All because I foolishly admitted to having 'O' Level French!

'I think we deserve a break' braved our pet punk after one hour's trek through Les Tuileries at 35 degrees centigrade in the midday sun.

With little persuasion we all agreed to head for the nearest café. I was unaware that the flock instinct could entice me into being a lily-livered 'yes' person. I was somehow persuaded out of my favourite gin and tonic and into a large glass of cold beer, which always gives me wind. But I realised, as I eased the weight off my aching feet, that these trips are part of self-development for your husband, your leg muscles and your self-realisation.

Back to the other half in my life. He was expected to return to the hotel about 6pm, after his all-day conference with a businessman's lunch and refreshments. He arrived half an hour early and caught me sitting propped up like a wilting agapanthus in an undersized bath, trying to massage my heel to ease the blisters.

'So, shall we pop out and see a bit before dinner?' he asked hopefully, ignoring the drained look on my face.

I hopped dutifully into my leggings without so much as a whimper, plastered up the blisters and painted on a smile.

'There's a nice little bar round the corner, would you like a glass of wine?' I suggested weakly.

'I'd rather walk around a bit if you don't mind. Can't come to Paris and not see any of it,' he replied with unusual eagerness.

We headed off at great speed in the direction of Montmartre, only to be accosted at the front door of the hotel by the larger than life wife of Mr. Boss, calculatingly blocking our exit.

'Oh, my dears, where are you gadding off to? John is taking his nap. Would you mind awfully if I tagged along with you?'

That evening I was more than glad to sit down to a real French meal complete with garlicky butter, oozing cheeses and baskets of bread. This was better. This was what I had come here for.

'What wouldn't I give right now for a plain slice of meat and a boiled potato?' whined a Norwegian husband.

My jaw dropped in astonishment.

Day Three followed Day Two in much the same vein, but saw a gentle shift of mood.

When sore Sunday morning eyes met over the breakfast table on our last morning, we found ourselves recreating the hilarity of the previous evening at Le Moulin Rouge. And, you know, it felt as if the party had never ended. Maybe those bonds my friend mentioned had formed after all?

I must admit that Anne-Marie turned out to be one of the funniest, warmest people I have ever met in my life. Even the pink suited panther had a soft side.

All Part of the Service
Joanna Parfitt, English in Norway
Are service engineers all they are cracked up to be?

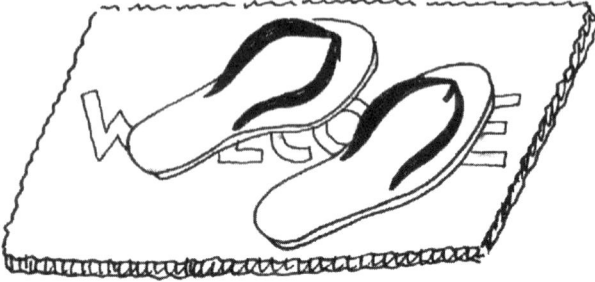

I have just had an extremely interesting conversation with a Norwegian wash-ing machine engineer about my spin cycle. Subsequent to my initial request he called me on his mobile phone and left a perfectly coherent message on my answering machine. He said he would come at noon. He did. He took away my washing machine and promised to deliver it the next day.

After eight years in the Middle East I can tell you it is a rare comfort to know that my electrical applicances are in safe hands. I spent years perfecting the art of shouting bald statements down an unfriendly telephone to the tune of 'Dishwasher broken. Problem. Come. Please. Now.' Only to know that the next step would be giving instructions to find my house. The following step would be to give the same instructions again. The next to ask if he had a pencil. Finally I would wait home all the next day and he would not turn up. Then when 'he' did finally appear, there would be several smiling gentlemen considerately leaving their flip flops on my doorstep followed by a lot of head shaking, a few bangs with a hammer, and then a desolate cry of 'It is broken, Madam.' Which, of course, I knew. Then they would troop off for a van, which would appear unannounced during the following week and then that would be the end of my dishwasher until I had found a way through a labyrinth of the service centre's telephone system to a man who always promised 'tomorrow In Shallah' and then asked my name.

I could bore you with endless examples of my experience with service engi-neers, none of which ever seemed amusing at the time, but in retrospect are infi-nitely so. But let me just share some of the juiciest.

Like the time our washing machine tripped the electricity in the entire house every time it started to spin. I needed to stand on the freezer in order to reach the trip switch. The freezer and trip switch were kept in the store room – the only area of the house without natural light. So I would blindly fumble and climb in the dark, find the switch only to be blasted back into darkness the moment the spin reached its peak again. Usually when I had just closed the store room door.

I wish there had been a happy ending to the story, but sadly it went from bad to worse. The tripping got so bad that we called in the experts. An expert left his flip flops on the door mat, balanced himself on the freezer and accidentally put two of the wrong wires together. There was a rather loud bang. From the office where my husband and I sat calmly tapping away at our keyboards we took our eyes off the screens and shrugged at each other, presuming the expert had fallen off the freezer. Then we saw smoke pouring out of the fax machine. Our computers died and all round the house similar fumes poured from the video, television and all electrical appliances that used power supplies.

'No problem,' said the expert, poking his dark fringe from his eyes with his screwdriver.

'Big problem,' we replied and calmly waved goodbye to several hundred pounds, replacing our power supplies and repairing our technology reliant life.

The expert scuttled off and we called in a man from the Ministry of Electricity and Water. He told us that we had 37 take offs when we should only have had 16 and went away to make his report. It never came but the landlord scuttled round with his tail between his legs and made our electricity safe for the first time in 17 years. Meanwhile our neighbours told us of the time their own store room had actually caught fire owing to the same problem.

Then there was the time our water was cut off for non payment of bills (plural). Yet we had never received one. The housegirl had a vague recollection of a brown envelope being thrown over the garden wall. The man at the Ministry reckoned that must have been the bill and told us to go and check our water meter in the garden. We did. It had gone.

'Oh yes,' said the man at the Ministry, 'You didn't pay the bill.'

He promised to send a man. He sent several. Led by an Iranian and with a collection of Omanis, Pakistanis and Indians in tow, they left their sandals by the front door, went out of the back and into the garden barefoot.

'Your meter has gone!' They declared.

My husband made an irate phone call at midnight. It was midsummer and without water the house was starting to smell. He was summoned to see a Minister the following morning and urged to bring cash for the unpaid bills.

At almost exactly the time water again coursed through our parched pipework, Ian was outside the Minister's office waiting to be summoned, the rials weighing heavy in his pocket. The Minister just wanted to make us sweat for our water.

Of course there was the time when we had too much water. It all began when a workman dug through the main water pipe line in the park and cut off most of

Muscat. With amazing efficiency, the blue water lorries, usually used to service the houses that are not yet connected to the mains, jumped into action. Within a few hours our small estate had two such lorries ready and able to fill our tanks through the pipes that had now rusted superbly from lack of use. The driver leapt down from his cab, connected the nozzle to our rusty pipe and started to chat. A few minutes later a blood red waterfall cascaded noisily from the water tank under the roof to the basement of our four-floored villa. The driver cocked his head to one side.

'No problem,' he said flatly, 'That happened next door too.' And he jumped back into his cab ready to flood his next unsuspecting victim.

Maintenance men are full of surprises too. Our most recent was called Ravi and it always amazed us that in three years no-one at his office ever seemed to know who we were talking about when we phoned. He redeemed himself with a moment of glory involving a snake.

The aforementioned snake had slithered into the playroom through a slit in the top of one of the doors. An obliging Sri Lankan maid with more guts than I launched at it with a broom and blithely bunged it in a plastic bag. Ravi came along surprisingly quickly, armed with an odd shaped piece of wood and some nails and neatly banged it into place, over the gap at the top of the offending French door. We never could use the door again.

Service takes on another meaning when you are in a foreign country. 'Immediately' is often translated as 'soon' while 'urgent' jobs are relegated to the end of the queue. The day you have planned a weekend away, the car mechanic goes sick and your four-wheel-drive is left unmended and forlorn. Taxis have no A to Z and fail to find your house when you need to go to the airport. To prevent an airport no-show you have to pick a taxi earlier in the day on a recce to your house. Then he has a good chance of actually finding his way back later to take you to your flight.

When we needed a plumber to sort out a blockage in our top floor lavatory we were naturally rather embarrassed. But our red faces fell as we watched him descend the stairs with the 'blockage' dripping from a plastic grocery bag.

Some service people are punctual and efficient, many are not. We became accustomed to shouting instructions, faxing maps and waiting impatiently for Mr Fix-its who either couldn't fix-it or never appeared at all. We saw tree fellers balance on the very branch they were slicing. We knew service to come with a smile, but never exactly as we'd hoped.

Today I am still reeling from the shock that my washing machine is to be mended within 24 hours of my call.

I can't believe that the Norwegian who is fixing it speaks perfect English and came at the appointed time. But it made me feel secure to see that he too left sandals on the doormat.

Flying Tales
Jean Exbrayat, French all over the world
In 34 years Jean never quite conquered his fear of flying.

I have experienced many interesting moments during my professional life abroad. I have sat beside a fully robed Kuwaiti local, who carried a falcon on his fist throughout the flight, and an Indian who brought his mattress on board and spent the time aloft completely engulfed in it. I have witnessed families picnicking in the aisles, old ladies having strokes and young ladies giving birth. I have flown in the Beuguet Deux Ponts that resemble fat geese and De Havilland Dragons, a bi-plane made of fabric stretched over a frame. I have encountered a Sikorsky S55 that needed several attempts to clear the runway when it had just five passengers on board. I have experienced crash landings in the desert and near misses with mountains but I have still found something to laugh about.

I love flying, despite the bad food and the small seats. Take one of those long intercontinental night flights to the Far East for instance. It generally starts quite well, the plane takes off hardly thirty minutes late, which for experienced travellers means spot on time. Flight attendants fuss around to get your drinks and a meal which would start a riot in a State Penitentiary, but that's okay because you are not hungry anyway. Then they show a movie that you've seen before.

That's okay too, because the screen is at an impossible angle and only one headphone is working. Then you try to sleep and wish you could lie in the foetal position. A man three rows back is snoring loudly. A toddler is crying. In the middle of the night you are terribly thirsty. You press the flight attendant button but nothing happens. You try again but still nothing. You decide not to make a fuss. They turn up eventually. Once I pressed the call button over Cyprus and the attendant showed up over Sri Lanka. So you decide to get a glass of water by yourself. As you have taken a window seat to be undisturbed, you disturb the others, who were fast asleep. After crushing a few feet and ankles you manage to disentangle yourself from your neighbours, creating a lot of bad feeling along the way. But at least you are free. Good to stretch your legs. You go in search of a steward. And here comes one of the very big mysteries of the modern world. They were on the plane when you left, at least a dozen of them. They have to be there somewhere. Surely all twelve of them can't be hiding in the lavatory? But not a uniformed soul is around. So you return to your seat to nurse your parched throat and keep pressing that call button.

As if by magic they all pop out of the woodwork just in time to remind you to fasten your seatbelts. They look fresh and relaxed.

And then the most disappointing part of the trip – my neighbours. In spy stories the hero always finds himself seated next to a girl who makes Julia Roberts look like an old hag. Not me. I end up with the 300 pound American tool-pusher who spills his bulk all over my vital space, or a smelly goat keeper freshly escaped from the Anatolian mountains. Once I did manage to sit near a nice looking woman. She had four children who climbed all over me, pasting me with chocolate and drenching me with Coca Cola. I think I preferred the tool-pusher.

Then there's the short flights within Europe that get me down. Of course the early flight is the one least likely to be delayed. It's just a minor inconvenience that the 7 o' clock take off requires a 6 o' clock luggage check-in and a 4 o' clock wake-up call. The plane is full of smartly dressed gentlemen with alpaca coats, discussing the merits of their BMW, tee-offs or their latest mistress. They all smell of expensive aftershave. Shortly after take off it's time to sit back and sleep off the early morning wake-up. But no chance. The hostess has only twenty minutes to distribute 160 breakfast trays and the duty free selection. There is no chance for you to slumber.

After a few thousand take-offs and a few million kilometres I can look back on all this flying and smile.

It is the fastest way to get there – but offers little more. At least the phone never rings, however . . .

Getting to Know You

Mark Eadie, English , now in The Netherlands
Some tips on country familiarisation.

An expatriate is honour bound to see as much of the country as possible. Typically you know far more about your temporary abode's tourist attractions than the natives.

In order to fulfill this objective you need a car. In most African and Middle Eastern countries this means buying a four-wheel drive. With so many expert expats to call on it is hard to make a choice. Some people (mainly British) swear by the Land Rover Discovery. Others (mainly Dutch) swear *at* them. Whether your vehicle is made in Solihull, Yokohama or Detroit, possession of your 4x4 entitles you to unequalled knowledge of the ins and outs of off-road driving.

The second step is to buy suitable or unsuitable camping equipment. Hotels are rare and dubious in many such countries. Suitable camping gear is usually only available by mail order from the West. Unsuitable camping gear is available locally. When it rained heavily during the post Ramadan holiday in 1994 in Oman and Dubai, thousands of expats discovered why their tents were so cheap. Again, when it comes to camping, the 4x4 comes into its own. With all that boot space we were able to take two kitchen sinks. One for washing up and one for paddling in.

The third step is to buy guide books and maps. The former are often hand written affairs, notes scrawled on envelopes or in notebooks. Maps are frequently considered to be state secrets, so the only officially sanctioned ones are on a scale that includes both the Equator and the Tropic of Cancer. Even when you have detailed maps, they are often of dubious quality. Maps in many countries are based on surveys done thirty years ago. Don't be too surprised when roads, rivers and towns no longer exist. On the contrary it is common for towns to be erased because of the presence of military bases or airports. As a result, guide books often contain no maps but have massively detailed itineraries, with instructions to 'turn left after 0.6km, then right at the orange bucket.'

Once the three key steps have been taken, the country is your oyster. In the Middle East, expats will travel for many hours, over rough and dusty roads, through monotonous desert plains, to reach a pool of water the size of the paddling pool they left behind in their gardens. If a waterfall is also part of the deal, it is remarkably easy to feel that you are a steely-eyed desert traveller, even though you are double-parked and surrounded by other expatriates, their children, dogs and visiting grannies.

In African countries, one travels to places where no-one else has been, and preferably in someone else's car. Five-Star Relay will not help you when your car is bogged down 210 km south of Malaimbany on a road last maintained when the French invaded in the 1890s.

One can find real treasures, and real disappointments. After talking about visiting a famous bottomless lake of legends, west of Antananarivo, for over a year, we finally made the tortuous trip, climbed for forty minutes, to find that the bottomless lake had dried out and was being grazed by cattle. A few hours later we discovered (oh yes indeed) beautiful waterfalls in a setting straight out of the Garden of Eden. Not for us the quick tour of Leeds Castle followed by tea and stickies at the Little Chef.

Several years later we visited the Ain Hamran site in southern Oman. The local guide said that the last people he had shown over the site were the archeologists who had discovered it. This was all the more surprising when we considered that this impressive site was next to a 'tourist' garden and picnic area.

When it all comes to an end, and it is time for us to move to a new location (new country, new car, new camping gear) I find myself thumbing through the guide books and maps. I think wistfully of all those memorable trips. Even the one when Tom broke out in chickenpox and Martha lost her dummy on that 1,000 km drive down to Salalah, seems like heaven now.

I always look forward to exploring another new country. Yet, as expatriates, we are not tourists, we are travellers.

I hope that in Holland we will find new untouched places – but hopefully this time somewhere with a decent road, a bar and a pool (heated, of course).

Finding my Ski Legs
by Linda March, English in Norway
Yes, you can be too old to learn.

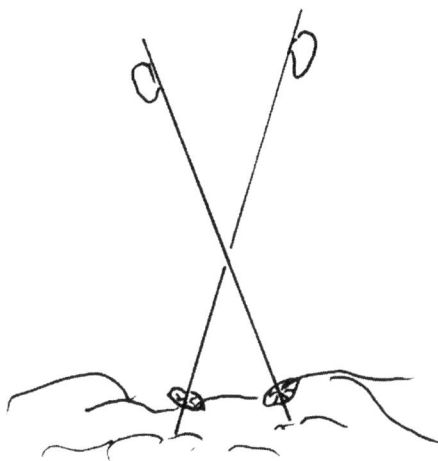

I come from a sheltered seaside resort on the south coast of England. We get snow on average once every seven years. Ten year old children are beside themselves with excitement because they have never made a snowman before. Cars glide into each other at 5 mph and are abandoned because we have no winter driving skills. Residents prepare for a siege – bread and milk cannot be had for love or money. Factories, offices and schools stand empty. The snow brings us to a standstill. It's about two inches deep and lasts for one day. In other words, if God had meant me to ski he would have left me under an alpine gooseberry bush.

And if things had gone according to plan, ski slopes and I would never have bumped into each other. But, as we all know, the best laid plans of mice and, particularly men, go oft astray and so my husband, John, arrived home with the news that we were being relocated to Norway. Until that point, 'ski' had meant nothing more to me than a harmless low-fat yoghurt. How cruelly innocence is dashed. Suddenly the word seemed to be on everyone's lips and no longer with a comforting black cherry flavour but with menacing connotations:

'Norway, how wonderful! Fjords, snow covered mountains – you'll be able to ski.'

'Who? Me? You're joking!'

'No, honestly, you'll love it. It's wonderful for the children to learn so young.'

Now, I'm quite prepared to accept that otherwise sane and reasonable friends of mine choose to mortgage themselves up to the hilt for the privilege of looking like the Michelin man in vivid pink snowsuits one week a year in the mountains of Italy and France. I've admired their salopettes, I've sympathised with cracked ribs and broken ankles. I don't laugh at that funny little suntan that stops at the chin. Live and let live is my motto, just don't expect me to join in.

My adamance that I am a born and bred seaside holiday-maker and not a ski slope holiday-maker held out for almost four months after our move until it became apparent that in Norway ski-ing has nothing to do with holidays. It is an everyday occurrence and everyone does it. Everyone except me, that is. Everyone except me and my children. And here, of course, was the rub. Once peer pressure kicks in you've had it.

'Please can we go skiing, Mummy, please, please?

And that niggling voice of guilt . . . 'it's wonderful for the children to learn so young.'

Add to all this the half-term arrival of John's sister, her husband and two boys and I was outnumbered seven to one.

Fortunately the snow plough had been out on the mountain road and in the car park where we parked between house-high mounds of snow. As we trudged what seemed miles in the bitter cold to the bottom of the ski lift and the little wooden hut where you could hire equipment, I pondered the advantages of the transformation from Dr Jekyll to Mr Michelin – at least you would be warm and, more importantly, you would look and feel the part. It's hard to feel like a skier in two pairs of track suit trousers, a crocheted beret and a pair of Debenhams' woolly mitts. Svelte salopettes and snowsuits glided past us. I had an ominous feeling that I didn't belong here.

The first problem was getting into the hut since we had to dodge the constantly passing ski-lifts to do so. It was rather like playing chicken on the M25. By the time I'd made it there, been fitted with horrendously stiff boots which hurt to be stationary in them and goose stepped out of the hut to make the return crossing, I had the added burden of surprisingly long and heavy skis. I had participated in enough dare-devil activity for one day. I was ready for the après-ski but the slopes beckoned.

Both John and Martin had skied 22 years before, so they were the self-appointed instructors. Unfortunately, my mental picture of a ski instructor is taller, blonder and more bronzed than John or Martin, but beggars can't be choosers. Of course, ski equipment has advanced during the past 22 years as much as John and Martin's physical prowess has declined, so it was rather like the blind leading the blind – not a comforting image when you're talking about ski-ing down mountain slopes. They gave us a quick demonstration of how to stop by turning your feet inwards and so 'snow-ploughing' to a halt and then bus-ied themselves helping the children, leaving Sue and I to fend for ourselves.

I remembered the instructions and got on my skis easily. I had a momentary thought of the whole thing being a doddle, before registering that I was on a slope and shooting off at a hundred miles an hour, screaming for help and turning my feet inwards with absolutely no result, straight into a tree. Surprisingly I didn't hurt myself, the thick snow making a comfortable landing point, but I couldn't get up. The skis were ridiculously long and wouldn't bend in the middle so I couldn't get my feet flat on the ground. Finally, undoing the skis, I scrambled to my feet, determined to try again. But when I looked around the realisation dawned that everywhere was on a slope and there was no escape from shooting off every time I got my skis on. I bravely had two more tries but it was like riding a bike downhill without any brakes – not much fun beyond the age of about 13. John finally tried teaching me to turn round. But after one 90 degree turn I was pointing downhill, my knuckles white from clutching the sticks so tightly, in the awful realisation that these two puny poles were the only things preventing me from hurtling off like an out of control human snowball. The only option seemed to be to have hysterics and scream at John to take my skis off. Completely disgusted, he obliged and glided off, 22 years sickeningly falling away as it all came back to him.

I can't help feeling rather ashamed in the light of how well the others did. Of course, the children took to it like ducks to water and John even took the ski lift to the top of the mountain before the day was over. We were rather surprised when we recognised people coming down for a second time since John had disappeared to the top, but having dusted off the insurance policies it was rather like holding a lottery ticket on a Saturday night waiting for him to appear. Still, you can't win them all. He finally hove into view and slid gracefully into the dying swan position as we all cheered.

Ever optimistic, John thinks cross-country skiing may be more up my street, so perhaps one day I'll try again on a flat piece of ground. Maybe if I got used to walking about, turning, stopping, I would enjoy it. On the slope I had no control. As soon as the skis were on, I was off, if you see what I mean.

They were all addicted and two days later John took our older daughter, Milly, again. He says she's coming on in leaps and bounds – well maybe it's early days for leaps and bounds, but she's getting there. Little Elsa and I snuggled on the comfy settee, ate the packet of English biscuits Martin had brought us, and watched a video of 'The Snowman' - the way God intended us to enjoy snow.

The Carpenter Came to Call
Sue Valentine, English in The Sultanate of Oman
Some things seem so simple, don't they?

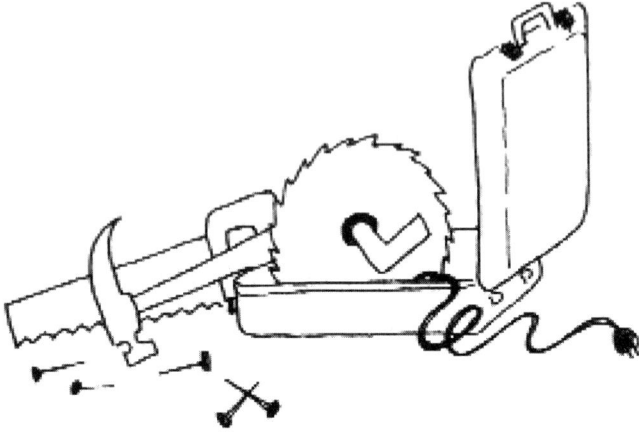

The recipe books were too numerous for the space they held on the counter, somewhere between the cooker and the sink. The books had been preventing me from serving up a meal onto four plates for several weeks and had recently acquired the habit of sliding sideways like dominoes in the wake of regular kettle floods. I needed a shelf. Time then, to call a carpenter.

Easy, you would think. But I live in a Middle Eastern country where the workmen tend to be paid little and are rarely fluent in English. A place where houses are all rented and we are told that all communication with the landlord must come from a male.

So, I asked my husband to ask the maintenance man to ask the carpenter to telephone and make an appointment.

The following day the carpenter called round at the house himself unannounced. I was out, of course.

'When did he say he would come back?' I asked Roti, our housegirl.

'He didn't say ma'am.'

Oh well, start again. This time I asked my husband to ask the maintenance man for the carpenter's telephone number.

I broke with convention and called the carpenter myself. He arrived at the appointed time.

I gave him a drawing and explained what was required – a fatal mistake. Never try to explain when there is a language barrier. It just gives you a false sense of security because you invariably receive smiles and nods in reply, which unfortunately do not mean 'yes', but instead 'I am very friendly and willing and would like to please you but don't understand a word you are saying'.

The carpenter took out his retractable tape-measure and measured. Twice. He failed to write anything down.

I asked him if he fully understood. Yes, you've guessed it, he nodded and smiled and said 'yes madam.'

Time passed. The pages of my cookery books were crinkled and glued together from a mixture of water and spilled gravy. I asked my husband to call the maintenance man who would, in turn, call the carpenter. Nothing. I asked my husband to call the carpenter. Still nothing. In the end I called the carpenter myself. I called the maintenance man myself. In time the carpenter did indeed reappear with the shelf, sorry that is not strictly true: he returned with a shelf.

It was the correct length – an amazing feat when you consider he had only to rely on his memory. It was round about the right width too – nothing short of a miracle. But the wood was rough and unpainted and there was not a bracket in sight.

I asked about the supports of course. I pointed at my copy of the original drawing, which clearly showed brackets.

'Coming, madam,' he replied and nodded and smiled some more.

I asked about the rough wood.

'We are painting, madam,' he assured.

True to his word, later that day, the carpenter's friend and his assistant arrived with a tin of paint. Three men with wide brushes painted my narrow shelf, then stood it on its wet end in the middle of my patio and went away.

Three days later they returned triumphantly with the supports. I think they wanted to impress me for they had already been painted. A different colour.

Eventually, the damage done to the paintwork, which had been caused by the less than clean concrete on which it had stood, was repaired. They even corrected the discrepancy in the colour. They attached it to the wall using the brackets. At just the second attempt it was straight – once I had suggested they borrow our spirit-level.

A year later, the shelf still stands. But today, when *Delia Smith's Christmas* flopped down into my flapjack, I came to the stark realisation that my cookery books have been at it again. They have been multiplying without my consent. I guess it's time to get my husband to call the maintenance man to call that carpenter again. Or maybe I'll do it myself this time?

Jacques in the Box
Sandra Williamson, American in Paris
Dogs and apartments just don't mix.

Only in France can our dog cruise the Mall, dine in restaurants, and sleep in the finest hotels. But in the beginning, life was quite different for the beloved Jacques le chien. He was not a planned nor wanted addition to our family as far as I was concerned.

It happened like this. On the morning of July 17th, 1995, my husband, Don, turned 40 and somewhere around 1.30 pm that very afternoon, he went completely mental. The day had started out very nicely. The kids were away at day camp, so, with the whole day to ourselves, in the most romantic city in the world, we decided to go into Paris and just enjoy being together – a rare thing these days.

We ventured off into the Samaritaine and went from one floor to the next, side by side, hand in hand (you get the picture). At this point everything was fine.

It was on the top floor of the Samaritaine that it happened. I can hardly bear to think about it. Their eyes met, they touched, it was love at first sight. I'd never seen anyone so taken by something soooo French! How disgusting! No, not another woman, I could have dealt with that, but a dog! Please. The puppy sat there with his big brown eyes staring up into Don's. Standing on his hind legs, in perfect form, he begged to be released from this most cruel bondage. If he could have said 'Take me home, sucker', I bet he would have done. Well, thankfully, the moment passed. I managed to talk Don into going for a burger. I assured him that our eldest daughter, Tracy, and our household, would be better off without a dog. I continued the argument saying how much trouble this animal would be in our small, fourth floor apartment. I reminded him that he is away all the time too, and so on and so forth.

For a blissful moment in the burger bar, I thought I was in the clear. We ate, made conversation, and were heading home when he slowly started gravitating towards the Samaritaine again. I knew we were doomed.

I reluctantly followed, praying somehow that the dog had been sold to someone else. The clerk, on seeing our return, and my husband's obvious interest, placed this puppy right into his arms and it was all over. They bonded immediately. Don had the same dazzled look as when the doctors placed his newborn children in his arms. I conceded defeat. Maybe I had under-estimated his need for male companionship in our otherwise female household. Neither had I, personally, given a thought to his desire to fulfill his eldest daughter's most passionate dream. We went home with a black and white fox terrier named Jacques le Chien.

Don couldn't wait to present Tracy with her new puppy. Tracy, of course, was eternally grateful to this Father of the Century who had bought her a puppy and showered him with 'Thank you Daddy, I love you Daddy' over and over again. Meanwhile, on the far side of the room, our youngest daughter, Tiffany, and I seemed to be the only remaining sane members of the household. The two of us stood back in total disgust while this puppy lavished Tracy in long lappy licks across the face. After all, Tiffany and I had seen this puppy and his tongue in compromising positions, if you know what I mean, and no way was he going to lick us! Tiffany and I kept our distance while Don and Tracy oohed and aahed over Jacques le Chien. There were rules made, and I threatened to throw him from our fourth floor apartment if he dared to do his bodily functions on my floors or rugs, and if he didn't get a bath at least every other night.

Later that evening, Tracy came to me with a solemn face and asked if I would really throw her beloved Jacques from the 4th floor, and I replied haughtily, 'Of course not, he could get seriously hurt from four floors up, we.need to be at least eight floors higher to really do him in. Besides, it's really your over-the-hill, impetuous, Dad who should be thrown from the 8th floor. But then, he is already housebroken.'

And so the Williamson household carries on almost as normal with one superfluous member. I haven't quite decided what the future holds for him.

Hold the press! I can feel something wet on my foot...

Excuse me while I go up to the 8th floor, won't you?

Housegirls Make You Fat

Joanna Parfitt, English in The Sultanate of Oman
If only Julie didn't make such brilliant biryanis.

Julie, our housegirl, comes from Southern India, and makes the most fabulous curry. Her biryani is renowned from Dubai to Muscat and popular demand has forced me to produce a small cookery book of her recipes! But it isn't because of her cooking that she is making, or rather 'has made', me fat.

Neither do I mean fat in the complacent 'I have much more important things to do than iron my husband's boxer shorts,' kind of way. No, I have become fat from downright idleness. It all began like this:

'Oh you must have some help in the house,' the hardened expatriate wives all chorussed at the welcome drinks party, their perfect suntans split for a second by a sea of dazzling smiles.

'I don't know how I'd survive without Matilda,' Suzanne said, shaking her head so that her gold earrings swung.

'There's just so much else to do,' added Hazel, laying her perfectly manicured hand on my pale arm.

It was tempting. No more washing and ironing. No more windows to clean or beds to make. But best of all there would be a built in babysitting service on the doorstep for Sam (3) and Josh (1). Living so far away from the Granny and neighbour breed of babysitter I would be bound to need a break. With some help in the house I would be able to write the odd article without one wriggling child on my lap and another asking why my mouse didn't squeak. There was even the chance to make a few pennies myself. It made so much sense that I found myself putting up an advert in the local supermarket almost before the telephone started to ring with hopeful candidates.

Troops of charming women sat, smiled, nodded and said 'yes, madam,' in my sitting room. I kicked shoes under the beds and showed them round, painfully aware that they were probably aghast at the current standard of cleanliness.

It seemed the right thing to do. The domestic staff who come to the Middle East all support extended families back home. The salary we were offering was like a fortune to them and I felt kind, charitable even, to be employing someone.

Julie joined our family, becoming Granny, Sister, Daily, Babyminder and sometime Cook. It took a bit of adjustment at first. Painfully obvious who was the most inexperienced, I found myself apologising profusely and walking out of a room if she was cleaning it. And I took to whispering in my own home.

But oh that glorious feeling of freedom: to explore the souks without having to steer an unwieldy double buggy round the potholes; to potter round the super-market without trying to squeeze a week's shopping round two crisp eating kids who both wanted to sit right inside amongst the groceries; to go down to the club for a swim without having to take two pairs of armbands and a blow-up croco-dile. And with Julie looking after the children, instead of my mother-in-law, I did-n't feel guilty. After all, I was actually paying her. It made it all the easier to stay a teensy bit longer and enjoy a cappuccino in a pavement café. Then I wrote an article for Shoreline and earned enough money to pay for more coffees.

Looking after children, carrying toddlers upstairs, scrubbing the floor and hanging out the washing had kept me fit. I had burned more calories staying at home than out of it. Sadly my favourite way of earning money, writing, broad-ened my behind more than my mind. But what the heck, I deserved a Julie. Living away from family, friends and fields deserved some compensation. I just slapped on some more suntan oil, met my husband for lunch at the poolside tav-erna and lapped up the high-life. Along came our club sandwiches - and the calories.

Hey ho, that wasn't so drastic. At least there was a simple solution. I left the kids with Julie and trudged off to the gym. Spent a few Rials on the latest lycra leotard and started stepping, stretching, toning and doing unimaginable things with weights and lengths of blue plastic rubber. Once I stopped hurting, it was almost fun. Lots of laughs in the class, made friends. I splashed out and bought a season ticket. And just as the kilogrammes started to disappear so did my resolve. It must have had something to do with that coffee we always went for after the class. Or the croissant. I told myself I'd work extra hard to burn it off next time. Only I didn't.

I felt good. My skin was glowing, but the pounds remained. The ones that attached themselves to my buttocks and thighs, that is. The other, sterling kind, were slipping away like sand through my lightly tanned fingers.

Reluctantly I unwrapped those same fingers from my coffee cup and used them for counting. I was paying for Julie, her visa, her bi-annual air ticket not to mention Christmas and birthday bonuses and gratuity. Then there were exer-cise classes and the post aerobic drinks. This exercise lark was not cheap. Nor were the latest Reeboks, leotards and floppy socks. And what's more to the point I was still fat. Happy maybe, but that cellulite was moving more slowly than my cheque book. For every hour in the gym I spent another 14 sitting on my backside.

I took the plunge and decided to spend yet more money. More an investment really, buying my own step and the video to go with it. Opting to cut down on both fat and spending - I would exercise at home.

The next morning I wriggled into my black body suit.

'Mummy, what are you wearing?' asked Sam as he lifted his jammy hands to be picked up.

'My exercise clothes.'

'You look like Batman. Dinner dinner dinner dinner Batman. Can you fly?' He started to wheel round the room.

'Just let me do some exercises, darling. There's a video. I'll put this on and you can join in.' I placed the tape into the player.

'But I want to watch Pingu.' Sam put his jammy finger on the eject button.

'Just let Mummy do her tape first.' I wheedled. And even as I suggested it resolved to add a second television and video to that burgeoning shopping list.

Five minutes into the tape Julie came in with the Hoover. Then Suzanne called to tell me about a ladies' lunch club. I couldn't win. Or get thin.

My house was spotless. The children were happy and cared for. The laundry basket was empty and the cushions plumped. I began to tap my fingertips on the coffee table as I fathomed what to do next. My long nails, unused to a life of leisure, made a harsh, hollow sound. Sacking Julie was the obvious step. After all, hiring her had been the start of my demise. But I could hardly do that, could I? My children would be disconsolate without their playmate. My husband would miss his biryani and scores of Indians would lose their livelihood. And I would shuffle from the PC back into the playroom and lose my source of income too. There was no going back.

I made myself a black coffee and took a celery stick out of the fridge.

Flicking through a magazine I soon found an advertisement for a local beauty salon. If I couldn't beat the system I'd have to join it. I booked my first manicure.

Article first appeared in Lloyds Bank Shoreline Magazine
Cartoon reproduced with their permission

The Fine Art of Haggling

Mark Eadie, English in Madagscar and the Sultanate of Oman
When shopping can be fun – even for a man.

Mark's Guide to Haggling

- Haggle everywhere - except McDonalds and Burger King.

- If the shopkeeper is smiling, you are being over-charged.

- If he calls you my friend he means exactly that.

- Walk away many times, complain that you have seen better across the road maybe even come back a few times over a few months.

- Beware of free offers - if you buy this I will give you four Chinese tyres free.

- When the seller starts sweating or starts working out complicated sums on a calculator, he is toying with you.

- Stay in check with reality. Genuine Persian carpets never have 'Made in Portugal' on them; wooden CD racks cannot be antique; the shopkeeper is not just being kind when he offers you a can of 7up.

- The phrase 'for you.' is said to everyone who passes by.

Consumer choice is an expectation for Europeans in particular. The luxury of being able to compare brands and models in one store needs to be left behind when one departs for the Middle East or Africa.

For many, many centuries shopping in the Arab and African world has centred on the *souk* or market. One street will have all the gold-sellers, frequently called the Street of Gold-sellers, surprisingly enough. Another will have all the spice merchants, another the carpet-dealers, and so on. The astute shopper can quickly check out which shops have the bargains, and can jump backwards and forwards between sellers, arguing the price. This haggling, often within sight of other sellers, helps keep the price in check. If you do not like haggling, take plenty of money.

Many goods are sold by only one agent or dealer, so if you want to compare different makes you will have to go to different dealers. This was no problem in the old days when all the shops were in the souk. Now, the dealers will be spread out all over the town, and comparing an Aiwa TV with a Panasonic TV may mean a 30 minute hike through traffic to another part of town. If you have more than a couple of brands in mind, expect to spend a month getting to all the dealers. In any one showroom, you will be able to see everything made by Panasonic, from fax machines to air-conditioners, but getting to the lowest price requires you first to decide exactly what you want.

On the other hand, very basic items, or the slightly obscure, can take on Grail-like searches. We once needed a jubilee clip for a garden hose. For more than six months we checked in likely shops, all over Madagascar. Not a chance. Then suddenly, in a sedate and leafy suburb we stumbled upon a small warehouse that sold virtually nothing but jubilee clips.

We spent nine months trying to find something to stop woodworm. By the time we found it, it was too late.

Sometimes, the best bargains are the ones to be avoided most of all. For years, the cheapest tyres in Madagascar were Chinese-made and did not fit a single vehicle ever imported to the country.

But whatever you want, negotiate the price. The newcomer to 'market negotiation' is usually filled with apprehension about haggling. A New Zealander friend refuses, to this day, to haggle, explaining that she would hate to lose those smiles and handshakes whenever she goes shopping in the market. She pointed out that stall holders come out to greet her in the street and welcome her with open arms. There is a reason for this, Alison.

Recognise that you will never win at the bargaining game. This is a cultural end-game that was perfected during the Pre-Cambrian era. We managed to get a carpet down from 1700 Dirhams to 380 Dirhams over three days. The seller was almost in tears as we paid, and we felt a bit glum as we drove off. Had we exploited the poor guy? I looked in the mirror as I pulled out and saw him and his mate grinning away.

Minding Language
Christine Yates, English in Germany
Language slip ups.

As adults, how do we proceed from no knowledge of a language to its full comprehension and application? There are stages. First, you have to banish any feelings of embarrassment; second, you have to listen to how the natives speak and mimic them; and third, you have to apply what you have learnt in a real situation. This sounds good in practice but can produce howlers of legndary size. Here are two, for which, unfortunately, I have become famous. My husband, David, bilingual in German, has dined out on these bloomers.

Mimicry does not always work. After long minutes of hovering around the deli counter in a supermarket, trying to think how I might ask for what I wanted and get it – a feat I had so far never accomplished – a German lady came to the counter, and, speaking clearly, asked for four slices of peppered salami and received what she wanted.

'That worked,' I thought, 'I'll copy what she said.' So I practised a few times by the bottled gherkins then strode to the counter and announced my heart's desire. I got what I wanted too.

Unable to contain my pride in executing alone and successfully the simplest of domestic tasks, I relayed all gloriously to a beaming husband.

'But what exactly did you say?' he asked.

Smiling exultantly I told him.

'You cannot have said that!' he said, falling backwards off his chair.

'I did, I really did,' I insisted.

Pride came before a fall. David collapsed in a heap and when he had composed himself informed me that I had asked for four peppered portions of rather embarrassing slices of the female anatomy. I never returned to that shop again.

My language skills eventually improved so much that I could be gainfully employed and began working for the British Consulate in Frankfurt. There was lots of contact with rather serious and status-conscious German government officials. I soon fell into the swing of the language and rattled on at a rate of knots, my accent was good and belied the short time I had been really speaking the language. Nevertheless, now and again an English sound would pop out in the middle of a German sentence, with the most embarrassing consequences.

One day I was calling a female senior Government official within the prison service.

'Good Morning, my name is Christine Yates and I'm calling from the British Consulate. It has been a little difficult reaching you this morning, so before we go any further could you tell me whether you have diarrorhea?'

I heard myself say it and frantically tried to put my tongue into rewind. The silence at the other end of the phone was ear-splitting.

I had meant to say 'direct dial extension' but pronounced an *f* instead of a *v*. Fortunately she forgave me.

Norsk Trouble

Paul Cleary, English in Norway
More Language Slip Ups.

The Norwegian language is a rare treasure, spoken only by four million Norwegians and a handful of outsiders. To the rest of the world (except maybe the odd Swede) it is completely incomprehensible. Actually, that's not quite true because Teutons and Anglo Saxons can decipher some written Norwegian, but the spoken language remains about as understandable as Mandarin Chinese. Present day Norwegian has its origins in Danish, German and MTV, and has, in contrast to many other languages, a remarkably simple grammar. Verbs are not declined, all letters are pronounced and adjectives do not have to agree to the gender of the noun they are describing. The difficulty comes in the pronunciation. Tones and double tones together with intonation on parts of words and sentences that are painful to the anglophile ear make Norwegian very difficult for the beginner.

Norwegian has about 60,000 words in everyday use. This compares to about 200,000 in England and 3,000,000 in Italian. It also has three more letters than we do, namely Å, Æ and Ø which are very difficult to describe to my English colleagues on the phone when spelling out customers' names. There is also a second version of the Norwegian language called Nynorsk or New Norwegian. It is taught in schools and appears on official documents but is only spoken regularly in certain parts of the country. As an ignorant foreigner I cannot really see the point of two official languages for four million people. Yes, I know the Swiss have four languages but the only indigenous one is Romansch and that's only spoken by one percent of the population.

Now back to philology for beginners. The Norwegian language holds many pitfalls for the novice. The verb *å love* for example does not mean to love but to promise. Much care is needed here, especially if you're trying to tell a female Norwegian customer,

'It will be on your desk tomorrow morning, that I can promise you.'

One thing I have noticed in the decade I have been here is how anglicised Norwegian is becoming. The influence of pop music, advertisements and, not least, cable TV, have left their mark on the language. Words like 'yees!, 'cool' and 'Libresse invisible' (oops sorry, that is French) have crept into the daily use of the modern Viking. If it keeps up at this rate then I had better step up my night classes, otherwise the language will be obsolete before I have had a chance to learn it properly. I read recently that more and more foreign words are being officially accepted into the Norwegian language. Many of them are computer and technology related, such as platform, overhead and software. But they are not accepted with the original spelling. If they were the locals would never be able to pronounce them. The Norwegians cannot, for example, pronounce steak, baguette or pommes frites, but then the English can't pronounce Reims or Dordogne either.

In fact, there is not much incentive to learn it anyway because most Norwegians speak excellent English . . . apart from the lady I met the first week I was here . . . I was parking my car and asked her how much the parking fees were.

'Well, you know it's very cheap,' she explained, 'You can have one time for 5 kroner or three times for 10 kroner!' I must explain that I know now that *time* (pronounced teemer) is Norwegian for hour, but at the time I blushed to the roots of my hair and presumed I had stupidly mistaken a brothel for a car park.

There was also the case of the English secretary who could not understand why so much money was being paid to a man called Per Diem. Incidentally, Per is a common name here, meaning Peter. This same secretary also addressed all the mail in one company to a guy called Med Hilsen. After all, she had seen his name at the end of all their correspondence. However, *Med Hilsen* is Norwegian for with greetings!

Bingo in Bangkok
Carol Mackenzie, Scottish in Thailand
Language Teaching is Just a Game.

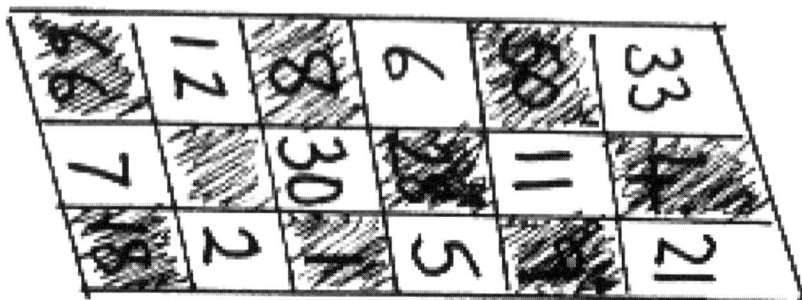

One week into an intensive course of Teaching English as a foreign language I was faced with a class of 12 Italian teenage boys. Although their command of English was elementary, their ability to intimidate a new female teacher was very advanced. It was as necessary to maintain classroom management and contain boisterous behaviour as to further English language development. Suddenly I felt enormous empathy with the French *assistante* we'd had at school, remembering the time we'd all mysteriously lost our pens and couldn't copy down anything she wrote on the board. By the end of the course my head was overflowing with teaching techniques, grammar, communicative activities and an array of measures to calm disruptive adolescents. You can guess which was the most useful.

A few weeks later, I arrived in Bangkok and was employed by a company specialising in in-house language training. This involved teaching all over the city. It was a major challenge to find the location on the map and fight my way through the chaotic traffic in the heat and arrive on time.

Fresh from my training course, I was enthusiastic and confident. However, I soon discovered that the cultural differences between myself and my students made some of my teaching skills inappropriate. Thai students tend not to ask questions or put forward their own opinions. They can feel uncomfortable if asked to speak out in class or take part in a discussion.

I quickly understood the importance of not allowing anyone to be made to look small in front of others. Social position and job hierarchy are important in Thai culture. A subordinate would not want to be better at English than his superiors in the class. If I called upon someone to correct his boss's mistake then I would be making the subordinate cause the superior to lose face in front of the whole class. It would be better to split the class into small groups of equivalent job status.

Thais tend to avoid giving bad news or causing any kind of conflict. This is because they do not want to be responsible for upsetting another person. Once I asked a class if we could meet on Tuesday instead of Thursday. Everyone seemed to agree and I was puzzled to receive a call the next day from someone outside the class telling me that Thursday was not suitable. In this way they had spared disappointing and upsetting me and the matter would not be spoken about again. As a teacher, I had ways of checking if they had understood the lessons, which was fortunate because it was unusual for anyone to tell me outright that they hadn't understood something. They would all nod their heads convincingly and smile. I wondered why nobody handed in a homework assignment until I discovered they hadn't understood what I wanted them to do.

Anyone who has been to Thailand knows how much the Thais like to have fun. *Sanuk,* the Thai word for fun, was one of the the the first words I learnt. Making English sanuk was the best way of gaining their respect and getting over their inhibitions about actually speaking English. One of my most successful classes was a voluntary English club held at lunchtime in a large pharmaceutical company. We played bingo. Each number had a question attached and the first 'house' would have no homework for the following week. Other favourites were Chinese Whispers and Twenty Questions. After a few sessions I was called in to the Manager's office to explain.

'Why are my staff rushing lunch to go to English club but always used to have deadlines to prevent them attending previous classes?' he asked.

Once I had assured him that no gambling was taking place all was well.

As well as teaching in-house English I taught small private groups either at my home or at students' homes. Many of my private students were Japanese and I soon realised there were many cultural differences between my Thai and Japanese students. A colleague summed it up by saying, 'Wear your smartest suit, arrive at least five minutes early and carry the heaviest grammar book you can find.' A friend turned up to teach a class of Japanese housewives wearing flip-flops. She was never asked back.

Learning English was taken seriously and they expected a serious approach to be taken by the teacher. Playing games, to them, was a waste of time. They felt uncomfortable when I suggested closing all books and dictionaries and having a conversation about the weekend, holiday plans or families. Their fingers would be twitching to pick up those pocket dictionaries!

Kissing and the Art of Keeping Friends

Joanna Parfitt, English in Norway

When do we kiss, bow or shake hands?

I have to admit that when Jeanette kissed me in church during The Peace I was rather taken aback. In our church back in rural Rutland everyone was embarrassed about shaking hands, let alone kissing. There they just grudgingly offered their hands to the people in the pews directly in front and behind and said 'Peace be with you' as quickly as they could before lowering their eyes and pretending to look for a tissue. Not in Stavanger, Norway. Here they walked gaily between the rows of grey moulded plastic chairs, shaking hands with every single member of the congregation. Apart from Jeanette, bless her heart. Clad in purple from her lipstick to her opaque tights, Jeanette laid her cheeks alternately on mine. It was as if she brushed my face with cashmere. Silently. No puckered lips. No smackeroo. A token gesture I suppose, for Jeanette had never set eyes on me before. I could hardly have expected a proper kiss, now could I? In Norway, it appears, they have perfected the kissless kiss. All show and no feeling. Like their mountains, so breathtakingly beautiful yet bloody cold. Yes, the Norwegian kiss is a sorry affair and their official handshake is sadly similar to the fish they sell and smoke in abundance.

Thinking of purple Jeanette led me to consider kissing in more detail. And no, I didn't dash over to embrace the vicar; instead, I contemplated the finer art of making friends and how important the greeting ritual can be.

When I left England, I was pretty reserved. A kiss for my Granny at bedtime. One for my Godmother. One for each parent to say thank you for a present. All on the cheek of course. Bang in the middle. Wouldn't want to touch lips, that could be classed as incest (besides, it was pretty disgusting). I had kissed my boyfriends, of course, and not usually on the cheek, but girlfriends . . . uh oh, there was another dodgy area.

Not that all English people are as tight fisted with kisses, of course. The Sloanes and the Titled that people the home counties and London do far too much of it. They kiss people they don't even like, calling them 'dharling' as they place cupids bows of pearly lipstick rather closer to the mouth than I would have dared.

I'd not quite mastered that sort of kiss. In fact I was so paranoid about getting it wrong when friends came to dinner, that I usually fumbled with the door handle and their coats so long that they forgot about it altogether. At least, that's what I told myself.

But then, as I said, I went abroad. At 15 in Germany, staying with my penfriend, I learned to shake hands with everyone in the room. It was formal, polite and not too embarrassing at all. Then I studied French at university and landed up in France. There, handshaking was strictly for business and strangers.

At 21, I found myself employed as a teacher of English conversation. Before long, I was embracing my 14 year old pupils in the High Street with ease. *Pas de problème* as they say. I kissed my friends and they kissed me, twice if they knew me and three times if they liked me a lot. I learned to kiss everyone I knew and shake hands with those I didn't when I entered a social gathering, and then to kiss them all regardless on the way out. It didn't take long to discover that what we call French kissing, they only save for their very closest friends of all.

Then I went back to England and found myself not quite knowing what to do with my lips every time I saw an old friend. Kissing wasn't quite done at Hull University.

Five years later, I married Ian, became an expat wife and went to live in the Middle East. There, I wasn't even allowed to hold hands with him in public, let alone kiss him at the airport. My own husband. But behind high walls and in high apartments there was a lot of kissing. Once on each cheek for anyone you came to know everytime you saw them. Not in the coffee shop, or by the pool of course, but at parties and there were lots of them. Kissing meant that friends became friendlier more quickly, and with so many people moving on after a couple of years you needed to make them fast. It was either that or stay lonely.

As the years passed I became so used to kissing that I no longer fumbled with the door handle at dinner parties. There was no question that kissing was only a possibility. It happened every time. Our circle of friends grew from fellow Brits who'd do it twice to the Dutch who'd do it thrice and even to the Swiss who did it four whole times. I'd look up just before commencing the ritual, check what number they were, and go for it with gusto. It made sense to go for the highest number, particularly as I came from a country who had no official number at all. I often wondered what would happen if a French woman met a Dutch man, would he defer to her paltry two, or would she rise to meet his three?

In Norway, I met a charming Argentian couple. They invited us to their home for coffee and cakes, which is what you do in Norway. No kissing happened on arrival, but it felt sort of strange, after ten previous kiss filled years, not to kiss them goodbye to show our appreciation. Elena put up her hand as I leaned forwards at the door.

'Argentians don't really do it, you know,' but she kissed me once for show. Carlos didn't care. 'I'll take two,' he said with a grin and dived right in.

So what do you do if you go to England, where they don't really do it at all, and meet an English friend you used to kiss twice when you were in Dubai? Do you still kiss them, now you're home? I think you do. And what if a Norwegian meets a French person? They both do it twice, of course, but does one do it silently and the other with a smack? Or do they both kiss the air and hope the other doesn't notice?

I heard another funny story on this theme.

Rachel Leroux, as an American, is used more to hugging than kissing. Big Macs, big hats, big country and big hugs. No soppy cheek-touching for them. If they do kiss someone, it's bang on the lips. No wonder they have high self esteem.

Now Rachel married a French man called Pierre and I'm sure she is happy to do it twice, or even three times with him. But one day in Paris, she met an old American friend and they hugged. Pierre's jaw dropped a mile, convinced that the hug was a sign they were having an affair. Hugging is apparently what only lovers do in France, not friends.

The Arabs, Eskimos and butterflies rub noses. The Germans, as I said, shake hands, while the other Europeans do a lot of kissing. Meanwhile the ones who once ran the British Empire, shuffle on the doorstep, flap their hands about a bit, look at their feet and then, if they're feeling brave, they kiss you once, right in the middle of your cheek. Only they don't know which side to aim for, and neither does their guest and so they bang noses, or glasses or both. Or worst of all, they end up kissing on the lips!

Saving Mangoes
Gurpreet Tirwana, English in Egypt
The art of flexible accounting.

Upon receiving the news that Simon was to be transferred to Egypt, I immediately set about finding out if my employer had an office there too. I was lucky - a few days later a fax arrived offering me a full time position in the Management Consultancy division of the largest firm of accountants in Cairo, paying a whopping salary of $300. Was this for a day or a week, I wondered? I dare not ask for further clarification. The fact that they wanted me, a foreign woman, in their midst, was exciting enough.

Being the first foreign employee in the firm, and on top of that, a woman, I became an instant object of curiosity. Of the 800 employees, 750 were men, so I became notorious as The English Lady. Every day I was there I was honoured with visits from people wishing to see how I looked and dressed, and those who wanted to practise their English. Accomplishing any work in this setting, I could see, would be a challenge indeed.

I set about in the way to which I was accustomed - keeping my head down, reading and digesting local regulations, crunching numbers and writing reports - only looking up for an occasional sip of tea, or a single exchanged pleasantry. As I had been trained to do in London, I maintained a diary meticulously, logging how I had utilized each 30 minute period of my day. At the end of my first month, when presented with a time sheet to complete, I was surprised. Keeping check of my half hours had been unnecessary, since there was a time sheet code for casual absence! Unforeseen absences were not just tolerated, they were expected and budgeted for.

I learned to work by the IBM Technique. I stands for *Inshallah* or God willing, B for *Bokra* or tomorrow and M for *Maalish* or never mind! Now I relaxed and spent more time observing my surroundings. A vast amount of time was spent each morning in effusive greetings between each and every member of the same sex. There was not one welcome, but several, and many enquiries about health. Each man would take the other's hand, grasp shoulders and kiss cheeks. Brotherhood between staff members was just as important as work. Egyptians have to like you before doing business with you, so my focus shifted to developing relationships with my colleagues, rather than trying to impress them with the sight of my bent head.

'The problem is that my best mango tree's branches spread out far beyond the garden fence, and little boys climb up them at night and steal my mangoes,' I was told in all seriousness by Mr. Mohamed one morning in reply to my concerned but simple 'How are you?'

I suggested that he put nets over his mango trees. He was delighted by my idea and I was treated to fresh mangoes every day for a month as a reward.

As I made friends, my advice was sought in all spheres - from whether a tie matched a particular shirt to how best to interpret International Accounting Standards, to how to write something in English. Before long, I ended up re-writing reports, letters and even CVs - several of them in my spare time.

I learnt Arabic and endeared myself by asking for help. My colleagues demanded to see the exercises I had done and insisted on helping with homework, albeit during office hours of course. They delighted in hearing me practise getting my tongue around difficult Arabic sounds, and were extremely proud that I was learning to read and write their language.

I quickly learnt to dress appropriately for the office and visits to clients. Out went my short skirted Vivienne Westwood suits and in came demure Jean Muir pieces with long sleeved blouses. It soon became apparent that my dry, knobbly knees and elbows were considered erotic. The chats I used to have about fashions on Bond Street with female colleagues in London, turned into talk of the different types of head covering available, and the fashion statements that each made.

It was difficult for me to work at times. Meetings I held were seldom private - they were habitually interrupted by phone calls and visits from colleagues, friends and family (not mine). My large office was often used as a prayer room - up to three times a day.

Despite the several interruptions to my day, I worked as well and as efficiently as possible. Three months into the position, with high profile successes behind me, I rehearsed my lines, plucked up some courage, and asked for a raise. I was rewarded with a quadrupling of my monthly salary. Being accepted as part of the office team was the greater honour, and much harder work too!

Recording It All
Mark Eadie, English in The Netherlands
The art of taking photographs.

The expat starts life overseas with a determination to record it all for the parents, the children or anyone stupid enough to accept another invitation to see the photos or video. We know there is considerably more to life abroad than can be found in Watford. Funny how the folks back home never quite share our enthusiasm.

It all began with a massive array of toys I gaily claimed the VAT back on at the airport. Camera, video, editing, development and display equipment, bags full of essential accessories that my wife never quite sees the point of. The graduated smoke-blue filter, for one. The labelmaker that will be a real boon when I find the time to sort out the albums and tapes. We have so many albums stocked with endless scenes of the kids up mountains, in pools, watching me repair a puncture, watching me repair another puncture, watching Mummy put up another shelf for the albums that appear to self propagate at night. Those bookshelves sag with acres of celluloid showing much the same thing.

Most guidebooks offer advice on what may, or may not be photographed. I offer a brief summary here of the many things I have discovered not to be okay subjects. Do not photograph airports. Do not photograph military installations. If the military hardware is old and unworkable the authorities are frightened you will send the photograph to a political satirical magazine, such as Private Eye. If the hardware is incredibly sophisticated and unnecessary, the same fear applies.

Do not photograph post offices, bridges or road junctions. Not because the authorities would prefer you to get lost and be unable to send a postcard home, but because your desire to take photographs of such items makes you mentally unstable.

Do not photograph religious buildings in Muslim countries, despite the fact that these are often of immense beauty.

Ask permission to photograph locals. This gives them time to pose and smile stiffly, then ask you for some money.

After taking a photograph of a distant village, we were once chased for 10 km along mountain roads by two locals. One leaned out of the cab of his pick-up brandishing a rifle. The other had his face pressed to the windscreen and waved furiously. Eventually they managed to overtake and braked in front of us. We stopped obediently. All they wanted was to have their photograph taken.

So now you know why so many expatriates return home with so many photographs of their children.

The Horror of Holidays
Joanna Parfitt, English in the the United Arab Emirates
Sometimes it is easier to stay at home.

It is round about March that expatriates working in the Middle East start to flag. The visitors have gone home and thoughts soon turn to the next vacation. As it gets hotter and hotter, 'Oh to be in England now that summer's here' is never far from your dry lips. It is not until you open your wallet to pay the airport departure tax that you remember all the things you promised yourselves the previous year. All those things you vowed never to do again. And here you are again. A glutton for punishment. Not quite as happy as can be.

Holidays take on a different meaning for expatriates. For one thing, we go away to escape the sun, not to find it. For another, a long plane journey with young children fills us with dread. And to cap it all, the highlight of our holiday will be living out of a suitcase at his mother's. You know the story.

While you are folded up with your knees under your chin, vainly trying to find a comfortable sleeping position in an Economy class seat, the memories return. You order another drink. You just know that your mother is going to blame your children's behaviour on your incurable housegirl dependence again. That she will smugly tell you anecdotes that begin 'when our children were young of course, we didn't have . . . ' In fact children have always been impossible when staying with grandparents for extended periods, without toys, friends or familiar videos. But despite the hardships, you still wind up feeling guilty about that self-indulgent lifestyle you lead that keeps them from seeing their grandchildren. You try and point out that your brother, who lives in Balham, never goes home at all, but that, it appears, is different.

But enough of Granny. It doesn't really matter with whom you stay or even whether you have small children, holidays can be one long headache. When you live abroad for most of the year, the trip home becomes a mad dash in an expensive hire car with a small boot, on the slowest roads in England, visiting people who were simply dying to see you. You've let out your own house of course. It seemed silly to forego the rental income just so you could selfishly use your own beds for a month. So you lug your belongings round like reluctant tortoises on a marathon trek that leaves you exhausted, dissatisfied and cross.

You can't win. If you try to miss out visits to anyone who only wrote to you at Christmas, sure as eggs they'll track you down and ring you up. They'll make you feel guilty to the point where you end up saying. 'Sure, we'll pop in for lunch on our way down to Cornwall. We had hoped to avoid the M25, of course, but we mustn't let another year go by, must we?' And when you get there you have nothing to talk about. Their children are glued to their game boys while yours want to play in the garden. Your friends talk about the recession and unemployment and make you feel so guilty that you tuck your gold bangles up your sleeve and talk about the hardship of not being able to get Greek yoghurt in your local supermarket.

So you book a last minute package to the South of France and escape the recriminations for a fortnight. The hotel is in a dark side street and has no room service. Your sheets get filled with baguette crumbs and the bathroom smells of camembert. The children go to bed before you do, but are sharing your room. After lights out you end up sitting in silence on the bed watching MTV with the sound off. Or you lock yourselves in the bathroom, drink Export 33 out of the bottle and play Travel Scrabble. You also long desperately for some air conditioning.

By day you discover that you have to pay for the privilege of a rectangle of pebbly beach just big enough for your towel. It's not the expanse of sweeping bay that you can't keep your eyes off, but the expanse of sleeping flesh. After the Middle East, anything less than a 1950's one-piece looks obscene. And the water is freezing!

You soon realise that you can't beat the beaches back home. By home, I mean the Middle East, and after a few weeks in Europe you are virtually begging to go back. Even if it will mean that the steering wheel will burn your fingers and you'll want to strangle the housegirl, that the kids will revert to being video junkies and your friends will all be away on leave. Or will they?

Article first appeared in Lloyds Bank Shoreline Magazine.
Cartoon reproduced with their permission.

Norwegian Holiday

by Elizabeth Douet, American in Norway

She wanted to get away from it all – but it all went with her

After a year of Nordic weather and nourishment, my husband, our three-year-old daughter and I were looking forward to discovering a bit of Spanish hospitality on our recent vacation to the Canary Islands. Visions of paella and sangria danced in our minds to an accompanying flamenco beat.

We all practiced our "Buenas Dias" and started converting our kroners to pesetas. While we didn't go as far packing our sombreros, it's enough to say that we were ready to experience two weeks of Spanish living.

You can, therefore, imagine our surprise when we found ourselves greeted with a resounding "God Morgen," surrounded by fellow Scandinavians, and served cordon blue salmon dishes in a picture-perfect hotel along the Atlantic coast. We had flown five hours with hundreds of fellow Norwegians to the perfect Scandinavian oasis constructed on the shores of the Canary Islands. Even the local supermarket carried more Jarlsberg cheese and ground fish balls than olives or Quaranta-Y-Tres.

From the start it seems we found ourselves in a bit of a cultural mix up, but things quickly turned to worldwide mayhem when we tried to explain what an American, married to a Frenchman and living in Norway were doing in a Scandinavian resort in Spain. Each time we tried to explain our origins, we became less sure of exactly what we were doing there. It seems hotel personnel couldn't figure it out at all as they sent us off at the end of our stay with best wishes on getting back to Italy.

Our initial doubts settled in when we all buckled up comfortably into our Spanair airplane seats at Stavanger airport. Expecting an initial safety message in Spanish and then English, we were told all life vest and oxygen information in Norwegian - and no other language. As we never mastered our "Speak Norwegian in 2 months" tapes, I started feeling apprehensive when the air steward handed me a safety brochure rather than explain in English. It seems his translations were limited to coffee, tea, or fasten your seat belts please. Each subsequent announcement had me wondering if they mentioned our cruising altitude or to assume a crash landing position. As long as the beverage cart kept rolling through the aisle, I figured we were straight on course.

While we booked our vacation through a Norwegian travel agency, we had never really imagined that we'd be transplanted to an exported resort. Our brain cells must have been numbed by a previous Winter and Summer of record cold Norwegian temperatures. All we discussed with the travel agent was a destination that guaranteed sunshine.

Dinner Party Disasters

With thanks to Elise Allen, Australian in The Netherlands
Entertaining can be entertaining.

You've been in your new country of residence for a few months now. Met a few people along the way and it's time to cement some of those relationships. You decide to have a party.

In our ten years abroad we have thrown many dinner parties, supper parties, leaving parties, children's parties, family sized lunches and brunches. We have enjoyed the excellent company of so many nationalities that I have lost count. Customs and cultures intermingle on the expatriate network. Non Chinese will gaily tackle chopsticks, dainty Brits will eat with their fingers and without serviettes and even the French don't seem to care if the pudding comes before the cheese. Such cosmopolitan dining has made our time abroad rich, interesting and hugely entertaining. Friendships have been cemented with more laughs than can be found in a bottle of Moet. Some of our best friends are Dutch too. A comment that will make sense when you learn what happened to Elise.

When Elise and Rod first went to Holland from their native Australia, they discovered that a dinner party was a highly complicated affair.

Soon after their arrival in The Hague, they decided to throw a casual house warming party for Elise's colleagues, inviting their guests to arrive at eight p.m. and to bring a bottle.

To their horror, the guests all arrived on time. Elise wore her jeans. The guests wore nice dresses and suits. They all brought her huge bunches of flowers and chocolates. No-one had brought any wine. She dumped the growing piles of flowers on the draining board in the kitchen and went back to Rod, who was wrestling with the cheese fondue.

They soon discovered that Dutch cheese was not meant for a fondue. The Gouda refused to become anything other than a solid yellow ball that floated round in a sea of white wine. Rod served the guests with their first drinks and then invited them to help themselves. They didn't, which was fortunate really because there wasn't much anyway.

Things went from bad to worse. The fondue was inedible. The guests ate nothing, sat uncomfortably round the coffee table and scowled in the direction of the forgotten flowers and chocolates. In desperation Elise offered to make some coffee and everyone brightened up. She had bought a really expensive jar especially for the evening, but no-one touched a drop. Eventually the evening ended and Elise and Rod flopped into bed not sure whether to laugh or cry.

However, the next week at work, word had reached Elise's boss. He called her into his office and asked her to close the door. He went on to suggest that she and Rod attend a week long cultural awareness course.

They learned a lot. Firstly, they were expected to only invite people to dinner if they had enough wine available. A good hostess should have as many vases as she invites guests. Flowers should be fussed over and arranged immediately. Dinner should be served at a dining table. Chocolates should be offered with the coffee, which should not, on any account, be instant.

Relieved that they were unlikely to make quite so many dreadful errors ever again Elise and Rod returned home to find an invitation from the neighbour for tea.

They put on their best clothes, bought flowers and chocolates. Arrived punctually at the alloted time and found the neighbours dressed in jeans, seated round the coffee table.

When we were invited to coffee and cakes with Margarethe, a Norwegian farmer's wife, we were faced with at least five different cakes and desserts to choose from. After a half hour which showed our hostess to be decidedly uncomfortable we had been expected to serve ourselves. So we did so. Then we were expected to do the same with every cake on the table.

Louise is married to a Norwegian and she has now become accustomed to the custom of helping yourself. She is no longer offended when her local guests help themselves to seconds before she has finished serving herself with firsts.

Belinda is South African and married to Chris, who is British. Soon after they moved into their first home near Gatwick, Belinda invited some new friends round for a real South African braii or barbecue. Again it was to be a casual affair and, as was the custom in her homeland, Belinda invited her guests to bring their own meat as well as a bottle. This may have gone down well at our Middle East beach parties, but it did not go down well in Gatwick. The guests were affronted to be asked to provide their own food. The barbecue was not a success.

Over the years the customs we glean from our foreign friends start to rub off. Since Norway, we now toast everyone at the table with the word *skol* and look them in the eye before we drink. Elise and Rod now truly prefer real coffee. From France we have adopted the highly unenglish habit of making a meal stretch to fit the number of uninvited guests who may suddenly appear as the food is served. We choose to drink jasmine tea with Chinese food and even prefer to use chopsticks.

Over time, expatriates learn to be flexible. They are happy to bring their own bottles, sausages or steaks. They merrily turn up half an hour or more after the allotted time, bring beer instead of wine, forget the flowers , open the chocolates themselves and hand them round without complaining once that they have been served instant coffee.

Departure Quotations

I never know whether to call the packers or the divorce lawyer.
Clare Ashley, after nine moves in six years.

I'm so used to getting a week's notice, that I can't cope this time, now we have had a month to think about things. I'm panicking!
Fiona Lonsdale, after ten moves in ten years.

My husband always tells me not to hang up new curtains. He knows that the moment I make that step we will hear of our next posting.
Véronique Kampmann, wife of Chief Executive Geco-Prakla.

Departing fills me with dread and sadness at leaving such a beautiful, majestic country, which is still filled with communities. I fear the rut of English routine which might replace my Great Adventure. I'd feel I'd given in.
Christine Yates, paling at the thought of leaving Germany.

I left with mixed feelings. Saying goodbye to a tax-free salary is never easy. On the other hand, when you've climbed every mountain, skied every piste and eaten every Toblerone, then the time comes when you have to move on to new pastures.
Paul Cleary, after Switzerland.

I was pleased to be returning to a real life and country with fresh air and seasons, long-standing friends and family.
Susan Valentine, after The Sultanate of Oman.

It feels like you have just seen an epic film or read a long book, where you became very involved. Great while it lasted and well worth it, but not something you would want to go through again.
Alice Hurley, after Norway and the USA.

I did not miss those cliques, that gossip and the way we had lived in each other's pockets.
Colleen Macdonald, after Trinidad.

Always Saying Goodbye

Nell O'Briant Bednarz, American in Australia when we started this book
but now in Venezuala

Boxes unpacked and kids in school,
I reach out to a new land
Like a beggar seeking alms.
'Friends, please. Lend me new friends.'
I cry, silently, among throngs of astonished faces.
One smile spreads to the eyes,
And I turn toward the brightly clad woman,
As the sunflower follows the sun.
'How do you do?' the inquiry begins,
The much-practised process of making acquaintance.
'I'm from India. My husband is an engineer,' says she.
We met twice, thrice, only to learn
That our recent 'Hello' must soon be 'Goodbye'.
She bids me farewell, heading from Brazil,
As I venture out once more,
Begging friends.

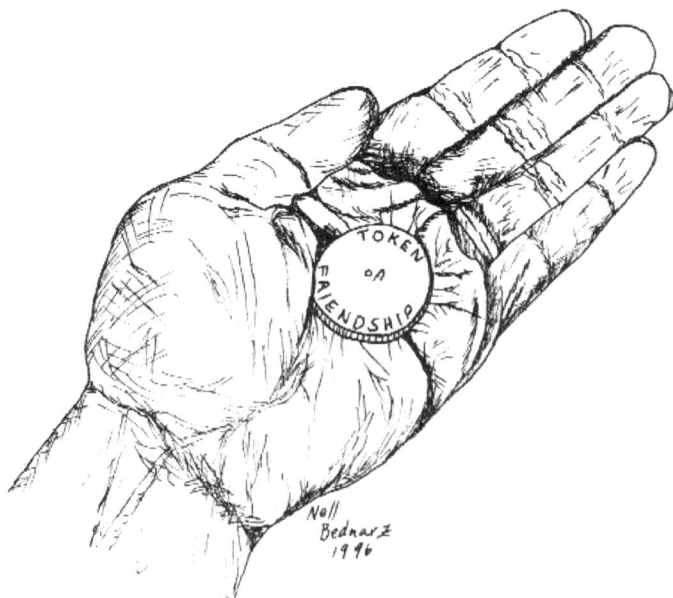

Remember to Stop at the Duty Free on Your Way Out
Mandy Taylor, Australian in the United Arab Emirates
A multi-mover's survival guide.

I know a lady, who, when informed by her other half that they were moving, not only for the second time in 12 months, but also to a 'hardship' posting, hurled the nearest available object at his head. Fortunately the object was a packet of flaked almonds destined for the top of a chocolate mousse. The packet split on impact, minutes before a dinner party. Later that evening, after several puzzled glances, one of their guests asked him why there were toenail clippings in his hair.

'I just wish,' grumbled my friend to me later, 'That it had been the mousse.'

Picture this. You're happily settled in Singapore, Dubai or Jakarta. The kids are in school, the garden flourishing; you have a job, a circle of friends and you know your way around. You've shown your houseboy how to iron a skirt, so that you don't look two dimensional, like the cardboard cutout of an air hostess, when you wear it. You have found the best place to buy bacon and Mother-in-Law's annual visit is over. Life's pool is fairly calm.

The news that you're moving on is like an ugly black rock flung into this calm pool from a great height. The concentric ripples spread to touch every area of your life.

First time around, the idea of moving to another country is filled with the promise of new and wider horizons. By your third or fourth move it can feel as though you're entering a tunnel. A long dark tunnel made of cardboard and bubble wrap.

There are few more dispiriting tasks than watching strangers dragging your possessions out. Again. In an endless series of numbered packing cases. With unemployment and/or divorce the only viable alternatives you just have to grin and bear it. Or should I say gin and bear it?

After surviving several international moves, from my native Australia to England, Dubai, Muscat, Bahrain and now back to Dubai again, I can tell you that although the official three key words are organise, organise and organise – my personal favourites are 'gin and tonic'.

Thus armed, I can drive the move forward most effectively, blithely promising the kids can have two hamsters when we get to Hong Kong and insisting that the owner of the windsurfer cleans it, locates all the dangly and sticky-outy bits or, at worst - sells it.

Plastic envelopes make light work of all those scraps of paper that are blown round the room by the air conditioner or disappear up the eager spout of the vacuum cleaner. Have one for quotations, another for lists, another for business cards and keep them in a file. Send out change of address cards before you leave. Not only does it mean that at least one person might cheer you up with a good luck in your new home card, even if it does have a picture of a happy snail on the front; it also means that if your address book gets lost for months in the box of Christmas decorations, someone will know where you are.

Have you noticed how you suddenly become invisible to some people, the moment you have announced that you are off? They skirt past you at the cheese counter, just so they don't have to repeat all the good luck messages they have already been through. Besides, you've already had your party. Hopefully you will retain a core of good friends to bolster you up and provide the ice and lemon after your fridge has been defrosted.

Moving day! Ah the sweet sound of ripping tape as a million singing Filipinos invade your home ... well probably not a million, but enough to make you rip large chunks of hair from your new, last-time-with-your-brilliant-hairdresser-haircut. They all have orange T-shirts bearing slogans, huge smiles, and they pack absolutely everything. Babies bottles with the milk still inside, broken biscuits, empty, lidless Flora tubs. Oh yes, every last Barbie shoe will be carefully wrapped, labeled, and turn up as junk in your new home. If you do issue instructions to anybody, make sure it's the boss man. My husband once issued what he thought was a fairly simple instruction to the packers, asking them to pack the clothes on one side of the wardrobe only. In the end he had absolutely no clothes to travel in. If it hadn't been for a pair of trousers inadvertently forgotten at the dry cleaners, and a neighbour's shirt, he'd have flown off to the new posting in his underwear. Yesterday's.

Somehow you stumble to the airport and arrive, befuddled and expectant at your new country. About one week later, your husband will be too busy to breathe, your kids will be at school and you will find yourself back in that cardboard tunnel, only in reverse. All the other mothers at the school have the audacity to know each other. You have nowhere to go on Saturday night and no babysitter you can rely on either. Now is the time to brace yourself for The Moving Row. A verbal fisticuffs that has you hurling abuse at your husband for making you leave your friends, house, cat, job or whatever, while he reprimands you for taking no interest in his career. So you take revenge by phoning all your old friends long distance and indulging in a verbal gin and tonic. Ah! That feels better. For a few moments at least. Until you realise that life is going on without you, that you will never visit the new shopping mall she talked of nor see Sally-Anne's imminent twins.

My last piece of advice comes from a lady I knew in the Gulf, who had moved 29 times in 40 years of marriage. She had followed her husband's career around the world.

'My dear,' she said, 'I just focus on the other end of the move, being in my new house, a deck chair in the garden, with a gin and tonic. I think about it until I can smell the juniper, taste the lemon and hear the ice chinking. It just reminds me that there will be normal life after the move. And then I take a deep breath and get on with it – sage words from a survivor.

Goodbye
Signe Hovem, American in Norway

A nod, a glance, a wink, a wave,
a stubborn smile perchance.
A clasp, a kiss, a hug, a squeeze,
a delicate embrace.

But goodbye, Godspeed, toodleoo, adieu,
so long, farewell are simple words
too hard for me to say to you.

Let me depart without the parting words
(simple words are so simple you see –
they cut like swords –
their meanings too strong for all
their meaningless intentions:
the time and distance I try to ignore
lie opened and exposed –
slayed victims of the valedictions).

So take your leave with a nod, a wave,
a hug, a kiss, an enveloping embrace.
Or look me in the eye – even whisper your well-wishes
but do not say the word 'goodbye'.

A CAREER IN YOUR SUITCASE
Finding the Perfect Portable Career.

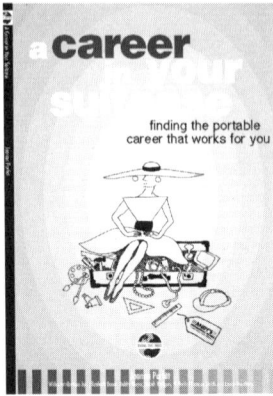

Chapters on:
- Skills assessment
- Working from home
- Networking
- The virtual expatriate spouse
- Ten commandments for a career in your suitcase
- 50 brilliant ideas
- Interviews with successful spouses
- Detailed appendix

A valuable addition to every mobile wife's book-shelf. Don't leave home without it.

Price £10.00 (+£2 p&p)
ISBN 09529453 04

To order this book, or to find out about forthcoming workshops or publications of interest to expatriates, telephone or fax Summertime Publishing on 0044 (0)1780 480304 or email summertime@lineone.net.

WORDS THAT WORK
An Association of Expatriate Experts

This association of expatriate experts brings together professionals specialising in areas ranging from careers counselling and distance learning to training and publications.

Do you live abroad or are you likely to? Are you responsible for large or small numbers of international staff and their requirements? Words That Work can help you to make the best of life on the move.

Putting you in touch costs nothing but could change your world.

http://www/website.lineone.net/~wordsthatwork
Tel/fax : 0044-(0)1797 225772
Email : wordsthatwork@lineone.net